MOVING A STONE
搬石

Selected Poems *of* YAM GONG
飲江詩選

Translated from Chinese by

James Shea and Dorothy Tse

Zephyr Press | Spicy Fish

Published in 2022 by
Zephyr Press   www.zephyrpress.org
Spicy Fish Cultural Production Ltd.   www.zihua.org.hk

Book design by typeslowly
Printed in Michigan by Cushing Malloy

The Hong Kong Atlas is a series of contemporary Hong Kong writing in English
translation. Established with funds from the Hong Kong Arts Development Council,
titles include poetry, prose, and graphic adaptions from established and emerging
Hong Kong authors.

We acknowledge with gratitude the financial and administrative support
of the Hong Kong Arts Development Council, the Massachusetts Cultural Council,
and The Academy of American Poets with funds from the
Amazon Literary Partnership Poetry Fund.

Cataloguing-in publication data is available from the Library of Congress.

ISBN 978-1-938890-87-1

CONTENTS

Translators' Introduction

Yam Gong is a singular poet. He is a literary outsider, yet respected across both experimental and traditionalist camps, among both older and younger generations of writers in Hong Kong. His poems may appear to be accessible and "friendly," evoking his widely used nickname of "Uncle Yam Gong" for some, until one discovers their sly paradoxes and sleights of hand. Even his slow writing process and unusual titles suggest an idiosyncratic writer: his first collection, *And So You Look at Festival Lights along the Street*, appeared in 1997 when he was forty-eight, more than twenty-five years after his poems began to be featured in journals. His second major work, *And So Moving a Stone You Look at Festival Lights along the Street*, was released thirteen years later and included selections from his 1997 debut. His forthcoming volume, titled *And So Moving a Stone (Hide-and-Seek-Peekaboo) You Look at Festival Lights along the Street*, contains both new and previously published poems, playfully illustrating that Yam Gong's books are really one continuous work.

The name "Yam Gong" is the pseudonym of Lau Yee-ching, and means, literally, "drinking" (*yam*) and "river" (*gong*). Asked in a 2012 interview by the poet Liu Wai-tong to explain the origin of his pen name, Yam Gong said he took the characters from a random Chinese poem, in which *yam* was the first character and *gong* the last. He didn't share the poem's title; revealing it, he said, would take all the fun out of it. Borrowing language to refashion as his own is a hallmark of Yam Gong's work. As noted by the Hong Kong writer Yip Fai, Yam Gong's poetry can be a heady mix of lexical registers, including dialogue, English song lyrics, idioms, lines from classical Chinese poetry, slang, and phrases from prayers. Yet the poet She-kwan once referred to Yam Gong's poetry as having a subtlety and quietness "like the sound of a clear stream heard in a temple,"[1] and the Taiwanese poet Yu Kwang-chung described Yam Gong's poem "Flying Ants over Water" as a masterpiece, noting that the poem is "magically beautiful and yet the language is so innocent and clear."[2] Yam Gong's knack for variousness allows him to be funny and lighthearted, and meditative and serious-minded, often in the same poem.

Born in 1949 in Sheung Wan on Hong Kong Island, Yam Gong is the third of eight sons. Both of his parents immigrated from Guangzhou province in southern China and came from well-to-do families. His father worked for the family business, a major Chinese medicine company. In 1949, he opened his own trading company, but the firm went bankrupt due to the British colonial government's ban on trade with mainland China during the Korean War. Unable to secure a suitable position, he remained unemployed for almost ten years. Yam Gong's mother began working at home, mending clothes and doing transcriptions, after her family's businesses, a traditional cake shop and an ice house on Hollywood Road in Central, closed down in the late 1950s.

When he was thirteen, Yam Gong quit school and began working. He took all kinds of jobs—first as a delivery boy and later as staff in a restaurant kitchen. As he got older, he found work moving heavy items, like crates of soft drinks and gas tanks; he was also briefly employed as a car mechanic. In 1973, he found a permanent job as a maintenance worker at the Kowloon Wharf, a large dockside warehousing site near Ocean Terminal in Tsim Sha Tsui, where he was responsible for repairing forklifts and cranes. By the late 1980s, when the wharf was completely transformed into a mall complex named Harbour City, Yam Gong was maintaining the air conditioning and water systems in the plant room, where he would remain until his retirement in 2021.

According to the scholar Lui Tai-lok, the Ocean Terminal's Café do Brasil was "*the* coffee shop in the mid-1960s and early 1970s."[3] While young bohemians and student activists gathered at the salon-like café, Yam Gong worked nearby at the wharf. For six days a week over nearly fifty years, he put in eight- to nine-hour shifts—both days and nights, with frequent overtime. While his coworkers gambled during breaks, he often read. Yam Gong has mentioned that he rarely sat at a desk to write poems; instead, he scribbled down lines during short work breaks and on his bus commute. Asked once if he wrote on his days off, he replied wryly, "No, time is too valuable to use it on poems."[4]

Despite his blue-collar background, Yam Gong is not generally perceived as a working class poet, unlike figures such as Tang Ah-lam (1946–), a former factory worker and taxi driver well known for his grassroots subject matter. Yam Gong's unique position in Hong Kong letters is evident in his distance from all literary circles: he has never joined any schools or collectives. In 1986, for instance, he was invited to coedit the poetry journal *One Ninth* only to resign after the first four issues. Speaking of his literary friends, Yam Gong has observed that whereas most Hong Kong writers dedicate themselves to promoting literature in various roles ranging from editorships to teaching positions, he would rather not feel "responsible" for literature.[5]

Although he is largely self-taught as a poet, Yam Gong did learn about classical Chinese poetry from his father. By the time he turned fifteen, he was buying secondhand books of poetry on the street and writing poems. His mother was an amateur Cantonese opera singer and a born storyteller whom Yam Gong credits for his interest in narrative poems with multiple voices. In addition to his schooling until age thirteen, as a young adult Yam Gong studied English on and off for about three years at a night school. In the mid- to late 1960s, Hong Kong experienced a series of protests over social inequalities: in particular, unrest in 1966 in response to a 25 percent fare increase for the Star Ferry, and riots in 1967 against the colonial government led by local Communist sympathizers. During this period, Yam Gong began writing poetry with a clear social consciousness.

His poems in the 1970s tended to be short and abstract with occasional images from nature that marshalled a revolutionary spirit of self-transformation and collective renewal. Some sounded like calls to action, as compared to his more searching, ambivalent poems from the 1980s onward. The present volume does not contain any of Yam Gong's poems written before the 1980s. One example, though, from that period—"Thanks," published in 1971 in the leftist journal *Companion*—illustrates the tenor of his early work:

I will be set on fire
I will be radiant
I will produce the sound of explosions
    cheering my rebirth

My song is of the greatest gratitude
Gratitude to the fire
and to the one who gave me fire[6]

Over a span of about six years, between 1974 and 1980, Yam Gong did not publish very much. Then, starting in 1980, he began publishing steadily in a new style, which has continued to evolve over subsequent decades. His poems became more complex and uncertain, and he started to marry colloquial language (Cantonese) with philosophical questions, extending the expressive capacity of contemporary Chinese poetry. He also began to rewrite a vast array of stories, idioms, and lines of poetry to give them new meanings. He won the Worker's Literature Award, his first major prize, in 1982, and again in 1984, and he received the Hong Kong Youth Literature Award in 1983.

Yam Gong credits his reading of European poetry, especially French poetry in Chinese translations, for the evolution of his style. He has cited among his influences Louis Aragon, René Char, Paul Éluard, Nâzım Hikmet, Francis Jammes, Henri Michaux, Fernando Pessoa, and Jacques Prévert. He once described Pessoa's *The Book of Disquiet* as his favorite book, and said that his own poems arise from a state of disquietude. His appreciation of the Turkish poet Hikmet, whose rich and complex voice he said he once tried to imitate, is due to Hikmet's poems about social movements that manage to encompass personal relationships. Yam Gong's interests extend to biblical language, and his poems contain wide-ranging allusions, from American folks songs, Danish fairy tales, German theater, Greek mythology, French opera, and South American fiction.

His Western influences are matched by an inventive engagement with Chinese traditions, such as folk legends, classical poetry, and Buddhism. He has compared his use of short lines, for example, to the style of Chinese calligraphy in which every stroke is clear and distinct. He frequently adapts traditional Chinese stories, including the tale of Xingtian, the headless warrior of Chinese mythology, in his poem "A Butterfly Flaps Its Wings," and the legend of Wu Gang, the "Chinese Sisyphus," in the sequence "Exercises in Fireworks." He also twists idioms and lines from classical Chinese poetry and draws on various Buddhist stories in his work, such as the Zen anecdote about rivers and mountains that features in his poems "An Occasion" and "An Entryway / A Resting Place."

Yam Gong's wordplay combines English, classical Chinese, standard modern Chinese, and Cantonese, a spoken form of Chinese used in Hong Kong and southern China. While Cantonese is used in daily life in Hong Kong, people grow up learning to read and write a form of literary Chinese whose grammar and diction closely resemble Mandarin. Cantonese is generally not regarded as a literary language, especially for poetry, but Yam Gong's surprising interjections of Cantonese in his poems broaden what may be considered poetic in Chinese. In "*Collected Poems from the King of Laziness*" (蛇王詩抄), for instance, "King of Laziness," (蛇王, literally, "snake king"), refers to Cantonese slang that means to slack off at work, whereas "Collected Poems" (詩抄) represents a term from classical Chinese. Side by side, they create a disjunctive effect that points to the humorous tone of the short poems that follow. Even as he explores spiritual or philosophical subjects, Yam Gong's use of Cantonese reminds readers that one remains rooted in everyday life. We find God using Cantonese ("A Song from Mother Mary and Miss Condoleezza Rice") and hear submerged voices suddenly speaking in Cantonese in a poem about death and silence ("Deep River").

A through line in Yam Gong's work involves wrestling with the nature and passing of time punctuated with the vivid encounters found in ordinary life. His lyric poems from the 1980s and 1990s possess a nostalgic lilt, but in a knowing manner that makes self-awareness of nostalgia part of the subject matter. He often examines time through the reversal of angles, whereby the speaker looks back at the self from another person's point of view, or from a different temporal perspective, which invites the reader to think beyond a linear understanding of time. "The Braking Bus," for instance, focuses on the various ways a single event could have happened, rather than whether it actually occurred. In "An Entryway / A Resting Place," a series of nested stories, the reader arrives not at the end of a "tale," but at a "seam" that serves as an entrance into or a point of rest in one's dream.

Yam Gong's poems span a wide variety of topics: meditations on memory ("Reclamation"), parent-child relationships ("Found Object (Urinal)"), social issues ("The Sinful Swan"), work life ("The Salted Fish Shop"), and quotidian acts, such as going to the doctor ("Back Pain") or preparing to kill a cockroach ("A Tolerant Person"). He has written numerous serial poems, including "Exercises in Fireworks," "Impromptu Poems 123," and "A Fox's Tale in Seven Parts," which are often brief variations on a theme. A number of Yam Gong's poems have engaged specific events, such as "The Subway" (concerning a subway drivers' strike in 1984), "Waiting for '97 and Godot" (related to the United Kingdom's handover of Hong Kong to the People's Republic of China), and "Tagging along with the Ascetic Practice of Silence" (in response to Hong Kong's 2014 Umbrella Movement). Yam Gong's style has continued to evolve. In the past ten years, he has been using his cell phone to "write" poems by recording his spoken lines. Consequently, he tends to write more quickly, and even more Cantonese expressions have found their way into his work.

The first book-length collection of Yam Gong's poems in English, this volume draws primarily from his most important work to date, *And So Moving a Stone You Look at Festival Lights along the Street*, published in 2010. At over 250 pages, the collection is extensive, and includes selected poems from his first book, *And So You Look at Festival Lights along the Street* (1997), for which he won the Hong Kong Biennial Award for Chinese literature in 1998. We have arranged our selections in loose chronological order, half from the 1980s and '90s and half from the 2000s, and conclude with a sampling of Yam Gong's recent poems that remain uncollected.

As translators, we tried to prioritize the rendering of Yam Gong's shifting tonal registers and represent his wordplay in Chinese, as it lies at the heart of what makes his poetry so beloved and unique. In "Back Pain," for instance, he uses the Cantonese expression *jiufai* (照肺), which has the double meaning of having a lung X-ray and being scolded by a superior. We translate the line as "Panic is when a doctor wants to see through you—" to indicate the power dynamics of a doctor's appointment; the later phrase "two lungs appear on the light box" alludes to the double meaning. A final example may illustrate the challenges and pleasures of translating Yam Gong's poetry. In "The Third Bank"—the title is a reference to "The Third Bank of the River" ("A Terceira Margem do Rio"), a short story by the Brazilian writer João Guimarães Rosa (1908–67)—Yam Gong plays with the sound of Wittgenstein's name in Chinese, writing it in different ways to create a refractive effect. Our translation ("When Wittgenstine passes through / When Wittgenstinestine and his language pass through") attempts to maintain this turning over of sound, which evokes the bending of light passing through glass in the opening images of the poem.

Before his retirement at age seventy-one, Yam Gong moved to Peng Chau, a small island in Hong Kong with a population of only a few thousand people. We were fortunate to visit his home several times, and always found it stacked with books waist high in every direction, with more books piled in plastic crates in his living room. Amused by our astonishment, Yam Gong told us, "Not many people are poorer than me, but not many people own as many things as I do."[7] He shared that he had never embraced Hong Kong because it had given him a living, but not a life. Although he may have found his values and his inspiration elsewhere, Yam Gong has given Hong Kong a great gift in return.

—*James Shea and Dorothy Tse*

1. She-kwan (璇筠), "The Sound of Dark Blue Water: On Yam Gong" 滄浪之音——讀飲江 in *Voice and Verse Poetry Magazine* 聲韻詩刊 25 (August 2015): 203.

2. Yu, Kwang-chung (余光中), "The Bauhinia Flower Reaches Towards a New Century: For the 2nd Hong Kong Literature Festival" 一枝紫荊伸向新世紀——為「第二屆香港文學節」而作 in *The Lower Reaches of Blue Ink* 藍墨水的下游 (Taipei: Chiu Ko Publishing, 1998): 143.

3. Lui, Tai-lok, "The Malling of Hong Kong," in *Consuming Hong Kong*, eds. Gordon Mathews and Tai-lok Lui (Hong Kong: Hong Kong University Press, 2001): 37.

4. Conversation on November 30, 2019.

5. Conversation on May 24, 2021.

6. Yam Gong (飲江), "Thanks" 謝 in *Companion* 伴侶 179 (June 1, 1970): 29.

7. Conversation on May 24, 2021.

MOVING A STONE
搬石

家常

大概四五歲光景吧
那年我病得沉重
迷糊中一個東莞女人
給我喊驚
一尺布、一碗水
一些穿戴雜物排在我床前火盆紅紅的燒
父母親在煙霧中走過
人影幢幢我的兄弟姊妹愁容慘淡
走馬燈般繞在床前轉
我看見我的靈魂
隨同我前生的小書友
到忘川嬉水

母親說
那時你真嚇人
全身冰凍
只有鼻翼
起伏在響
聽見賣白糖糕的叫聲
才睜開眼睛
淒楚地笑

後來呢，母親
後來你批判社會
我們遠遠看着你一天天

痊癒了

Daily Life

I was maybe four or five
when I became seriously ill
In my delirium, a woman from Dongguan
wailed for my soul's return
One foot of cloth, one bowl of water,
clothes burning brightly in a brazier at the foot of my bed
My parents walked amid the smoke
Through flickering silhouettes my worried brothers and sisters
spun around my bed like horses on a revolving lantern
I saw my soul
following schoolmates from a former life
playing in the river of forgetfulness

Mother said,
You had us scared
Your body was ice cold
The trembling of your nostrils
the only sound
Not until you heard the voice of the sponge-cake seller
did you open your eyes
and smile grimly

And then what, Mother?
Then you came to judge the world
We were watching you from far away, and day by day

you recovered

新填地

我已完全不認得了
新填地，當新填的時候
光赤的屁股曾暖洋洋的躺在
曬整整一季夏午呢
風的鹽粒，海的媚惑
加上少年肝膽
誰要是從渡輪上拋下一角
「噗通、噗通」的浪花裏
不用嘴銜着就不再冒出頭來
立志做野孩子
流浪，從一條駁艇
到另一條駁艇
那時，一帶嶙峋的石上
每當夜幕低垂，便站着
一個穿斑衣的
簫王，吹亮幽幽怨怨
一盞盞大光燈
便有生鬼七
鬼斧神工鉗一柄木鋸在二郎腿上
運弓拉着
一段段周璇
揀人擠的地方鑽
像一匹小鼠
在汗濕的脇下，尿濕的胯下
瞪眼便見外江佬吞大石卵
吐出來帶血
行船仔買金烏蠅

Reclamation

I don't recognize it anymore
this reclaimed land—when it was first filled in
my warm naked butt lazed there
under the afternoon sun for an entire summer!
Salt in the wind, charm of the sea
and youthful guts—
if someone tossed a coin from the ferry
you'd hear us plashing into the waves
emerging only when the coin was between our teeth
Resolved to be a wild stray,
I'd roam from sampan
to sampan
Back then, when night fell
the Flute King stood
on an outcropping in a spotted cloak
blowing a light into each
gloomy paraffin lamp
Then came Mr. Lively Ghost No. 7
bent over a handsaw and with an uncanny knack
drawing a nimble bow across to play
Zhou Xuan's songs, one after another—
I'd wriggle into the most congested places
like a little mouse
under a sweaty armpit, under a piss-soaked crotch
watching with bulging eyes a northerner swallowing a large
    egg-shaped stone
and spit it back up with blood
a young boatman buying Spanish fly

白鶴老叟放一塊塊磚頭在額上砸碎
用七節鋼鞭鞭一節節的自己
然後塗叫賣的酒藥
夜夜如是，五毫錢醫五勞七傷
一毫錢一片香口膠，嚼到
永遠，鐃鈸鑼鼓中
勞苦大眾都是落魄書生
揩一揩買涼果的花旦
生活便又平凡又璀璨
那時年紀小，「太不像話」
冒雨也去聽一齣齣鹹濕笑話
滿腦子顫動神秘的預言
神秘的掌故，甚麼老糠
沉底，大石浦頭
浪淘不盡諸葛孔明舌戰劉伯溫
驚奇的眼睛
隨一柄紙扇一開一合
逢人會問
「五百年前知有你
你今知道有誰人」
可從沒問過說書人格林童話安徒生
便這樣
縱橫闖蕩尋師學劍
直到一天晴天
霹靂，忽然大火燒起
燒了紅蓮寺又燒了對面
一幢三層旅店
燒死斑衣簫王，照田雞阿二
拆字問卜一群鬼谷神算

a grizzled old man smashing bricks on his forehead
lashing each limb with a seven-sectioned whip
then rubbing on the tinctures he hawks
Night after night—*fifty cents cures a dozen pains,*
ten cents for a piece of gum, chewed
forever, among the cymbals and gongs,
the laboring masses all down-and-out scholars from an ancient story
brushing up against a street opera actress buying fruit candy
and so a life is ordinary and radiant
In those days I was young and "improper"
braving the rain just to hear some dirty jokes,
head trembling full of cryptic prophecies
and cryptic tales—*dried husks*
sinking and large stones bobbing
The endless waves never washed away the contest between
    Zhuge Liang and Liu Bowen
With astonished looks
we followed the storyteller's fan opening and closing
as he asked every bystander,
Five hundred years ago, I knew about you
Who in the future do you know today?
but no one ever asked him about Grimm or Andersen
And so it was:
searching everywhere for a sword teacher
until one day like a bolt
out of the blue a great fire broke out
burning down the Red Lotus Temple and burning down
a three-story hotel across the street,
burning to death the Flute King in his speckled coat, the all-seeing
    palm reader,
the fortune teller with his cards, the psychic, and their fellow diviners,

唱歐西歌的塘西蘇小小
那一家大細茅山師傅
一家大細
無一倖免……
只剩得
一個企街姑姑，依然
企立海邊
生涯啊
教她相信
十八年後會重逢
一個面善
或不面善
的男子

Tiny Su from Shek Tong Tsui who sang Western songs,
that entire family of the Daoist shaman,
that entire family
No one was spared—
Only an auntie of the night
remained, still
standing by the seaside
Ah, this life
teaches her to believe
that she will be reunited in eighteen years
with a man
who has a familiar face
or an unfamiliar face

邊緣人

午飯後是各適其適的
趕七毫子巴士
撿一份雜誌
在懸想的顛簸裏打幾聲呵欠。

「有賭未為輸！」
劈頭劈腦
時常就有堅執的臉
四濺的泡沫
狼藉一地的
煙屍，和同樣零落的
故事，我又錯過了⋯⋯

設想
當你昂然撞去
見者不見
笑者不笑
恩仇泯滅
地球依舊旋轉。

時常
夾着厚厚
古典，薄薄
新潮
赴宴
拜年
且挨近過
煙波浩渺的
賭聚旁邊。

On the Margins

To each one's own after lunch:
catching a seventy-cent bus,
picking up a magazine,
yawning in the waves of a daydream.

You haven't lost if the bet's still on!
Those determined faces
often cutting past me,
spit flying everywhere,
the discarded corpses
of cigarettes scattered
like stories I've missed out on again—

Imagine
when you bolt into the room:
those to be seen are no longer seen
Those who laughed vanish with their laughter
Debts of gratitude and vengeance are obliterated
and the earth spins as usual.

Often
with thick classics
and skinny moderns
under my arm,
I attended banquets
and made New Year's visits,
having been so close
to those gambling
covered in vast smoke

相處
是一門藝術
孤立自己
如歌德所說
亦然。

記得嗎
我倆攜手
敢向世界挑戰
如今，挽着自己心愛
穿街過市
也算有了
疏狂的
歲月。

歲月，甚麼叫歲月
堅持還是妥協
熙攘人群中誰尖叫
一枚透明的　異端
百無聊賴地
存活，彷彿黑濕的枝頭
一葉
　　褪色的
　　　　招貼。

Being with others
is an art
and the same is true,
as Goethe said,
of being alone.

Do you remember?
Together we dared
to defy the world
and now, taking my lover's hand,
crossing the city streets,
at least I can reminisce about
those wild
years.

Years—what is that thing called "years"?
To persevere or to compromise?
Who's that shrieking in the crowd?
A little piece of invisible   heresy
whiling away
the days as on a wet black bough:
the faded
          leaf
               of a poster.

鹹魚店（十四行）

吊在那裏很久了那鹹魚
上工頭一天我用叉
把它掛起來我便想
這鹹魚肉質彬彬的
任誰都會揀去它吧
但它一天天吊在那裏直挺挺的
一丁點兒鹽也沒見掉下來
今天該有人揀去它了
每天早上看着它每天我都這樣想
我每天都這樣想這樣想
漸漸變成了我每天的希望直到
今天老闆過來跟我說
你呆頭呆腦像條鹹魚似的
明天不用上工了

The Salted Fish Shop (A Sonnet)

It hung there for a long time, that salted fish
On the first day of work I used a pole
to hang it up and I started thinking
this salted fish is so handsome
surely someone is going to pick it
but day after day it hung there upright
and not a single grain of salt fell
Today someone should pick it
Looking at it every morning I thought every day
this same thing every day I looked at it
and slowly it became my hope each day
until my boss came to me today and said
You look as dumb as a salted fish
Don't bother coming back tomorrow

於是你沿街看節日的燈飾

「人生不相見
動如參與商
今夕復何夕
煙花多璀璨」

回到家門口才發覺
丟失了鑰匙
有沒有轉動
門的把手呢
門的把手轉動的聲音
告訴你沒有奇蹟
或者奇蹟在屋內
你沒法看見
你的心想到一個最近的朋友
最近的朋友以至最遠的朋友
這一夜，都外出看煙花了
你沿街看節日的燈飾
你不大習慣每一顆燈泡
為你而光亮
你不大習慣
那些諂媚
多顏色的鐘
說服你單純的快樂
但你也哼出普天頌讚的調子
懷想掛在鐵窗前的襪子
漫漫長夜不知是囚徒的幽默
還是囚徒的諷刺

And So You Look at Festival Lights along the Street

Never meeting as life goes on,
always like the stars Scorpius and Orion.
Then what evening is this—
with fireworks so resplendent?

Returning to your apartment you find
you've lost your key
Did you try turning
the door handle?
The sound of a jiggling handle
tells you there are no miracles
or there's a miracle inside
that you can't see
You think of the nearest friend
From the nearest to the farthest
they've all gone out to see the fireworks
Looking at festival lights along the street
you're not used to every lightbulb
brightening for you
You're not used
to those fawning
bells in numerous colors
convincing you of pure merriment
but you join along with the joyful hymns
recalling a sock hanging in front of iron bars
on an endless night—was it humor
or irony from the prisoner?

但你知道最大的幽默
是當你回來
同志們都外出
今夜煙花燦爛
而你確信
要是他們知道
定會留守屋內
招喚妻兒
——介紹給你
各款牆紙
和快樂
而你的眼角有霧升起
知道雖然遙遠卻值得奮鬥
值得為此而收斂自己修飾自己
值得爭取
這每隔一段日子
被假釋的喜悅
於是你沿街看節日的燈飾
也漸漸習慣
讓節日的燈飾看你
取悅你

But you know the greatest joke
is when you come back
and all of your comrades are out
Tonight the fireworks are resplendent
and you're sure
if they'd known
they would have stayed home
and called for their wives and children
to be introduced to you one by one
amid various wallpapers
and merriments
and yet mist rises from the corner of your eye
as you know that while far away it may be worth struggling for
worth restraining and refining oneself for
worth fighting for
every once in a while
this joy of being on parole
and so you look at festival lights along the street
and gradually get used
to the gaze of holiday lights
and how they try to please you

地下鐵

聞地鐵員工罷工復工有感

生活的鐵軌
從地面
鋪至地下
歲月
"To be
or not to be"
無從躲閃

「安全島呢？」你說

在電閘的啟閉間
愛情
　　也分段
溜走了
長更
　　短更
長停
　　短停
擺盪的
　　　那節奏
擺盪的
　　　人呀
「仲等啲
乜嘢呢？」

The Subway

Upon hearing that striking subway workers returned to work

Life's rails
run from the surface
to the underground
Years of
To be
or not to be
Nowhere to escape

Where's the safety island? you ask

Between a circuit breaker being on or off
love
     also splits
and slips away
a long shift
     a short shift
a long pause
     a short pause
that rhythm
       asway
oh people
       asway
What're we
waiting for?

為要戰勝卑微
不跨越黃綫
是否
比粉身碎骨
可恥！
生活
有些企立的痛楚
較縱身一躍
更凜然
而無從見證啊

「係咩係咩！」

我想將感受
深藏
像受傷的
蚯蚓
但
泥土呢！
泥土呢！

Are you more ashamed
to stand behind the yellow line
or to be ripped to pieces
fighting against your lowly position?
There's more dignity
in the pain of staying put
in life
than in leaping
and yet, there are no witnesses!

Really? Really?

I want to hide my feelings
deep down
like an injured
earthworm
but
where's my dirt!
where's my dirt!

罪惡的天鵝

假使我的名字不是簽在支票本上
杜鵑花的花萼上
灑了香水的嘉賓名冊上
關於視野的天橋的位置的決議上
木結構橫街茶居的存廢爭辯上
蝴蝶雙週慈善香吻的統計表上
假使我的名字，我的呼喚，不關乎這個
不關乎一隻銀狐如何在冰天雪地中得到恰如其分的愛
你說，這難道就是罪惡

這難道就是罪惡
假使我爬上一枝傾側的桅杆
蹲坐在飄移擱淺的橫樑
因為暮色襲來吧，我傷感，我歌唱
我歌唱：垂危的都不要絕望
匍伏的試試站立起來
漂浮的浮去有岸的地方
你說，這難道就是罪惡

這難道就是罪惡
假使我介入不幸者的喜怒哀樂
而且捲起了褲腳
假使我預感某種危機悄悄到來
論證雨點有一天會下墮成火
並且將秘密一頁頁公開
你以為怎樣
你以為怎樣

The Sinful Swan

If my name's not signed on a check
nor on the sepals of a rhododendron
nor in a guestbook sprinkled with perfume
nor on a resolution for the skybridge site that will determine
    our scenic views
nor on a petition against the protection or abolition of a wooden tea house
    in an alley
nor on the pie chart about charity kisses in the *Butterfly Biweekly*
If my name, my crying out, is irrelevant to all this,
irrelevant to how a silver fox finds her due lot in love amid snow and ice—
tell me, is this sinful?

Is it sinful
if I climb a tilted mast,
if I squat on a beached crossbeam swaying in the tide,
if twilight intrudes and I'm sad and I sing,
I sing, *Those who are dying, don't despair*
Those who are prostrate, try to stand
Those who are floating, float to shore
Tell me, is this sinful?

Is it sinful
if I intervene in the joys and sorrows of the unfortunate
and roll up my trousers,
if I foresee some kind of crisis arriving quietly
and contend that the rain will fall one day like fire
and I leak secrets page by page—
Then what would you think?
Then what would you think?

假使你要我遺忘我偏偏戀上
你說：對。我說：錯
你說：寶貝，乖乖。而我
而我把普遍的權利放在普遍的人的手上
這難道就是罪惡

這難道就是罪惡
假使同情在批准之外
關懷流出了規定的方向
而溫柔竟是一種力量

是的，這就是罪惡，這一點兒也不誇張
假使一位淑女不是一隻天鵝
一隻天鵝不在掌聲中掠過
掠過的時候忽然轉過頭來
對着淚眼汪汪的人兒們
輕輕一喝——
　　　　　搞錯，搞錯
　　　　　垂死的
　　　　　在另一角落

If you want me to forget, yet I fall in love
You say, *This is correct.* I say, *This is wrong.*
You say, *Baby, behave.* And I,
and I put common rights in the hands of common people—
Is this sinful?

Is it sinful
to sympathize beyond what's permissible,
to care for others outside the given path
as if tenderness were a force of its own?

Yes, it's all sinful—it's no exaggeration—
if a young lady doesn't play a swan
and a passing swan is not met with applause
and passing by it suddenly turns its head
to shout gently
at the teary-eyed people,

> *You got it wrong, you got it wrong*
> *The one who's dying*
> *is in another corner*

飛蟻臨水

風雨前夕
就多飛蟻
父親說
端盤水來吧
哥哥便拖了木屐
躂躂走進廚房裏

我們看父親
跨上桌椅
解下鉤上的電線
把燈泡低垂
於是母親
熄掉別的
所有的燈
我們圍攏
唯一的光源裏
飛蟻蓬亂紛飛
我們一家子的眼睛
水紋上莫名地閃
莫名地笑

許多年過去
父親像一隻飛蟻
飛進另一盤水裏
而我們離開故居
許久沒聽見
木屐的聲音了

小女兒和兒子問起
是爺爺想出的主意麼

Flying Ants Approaching Water

Flying ants gathering
on the eve of a rainstorm—
my father would say,
Bring me a basin of water,
and shuffling his wooden clogs
my older brother would clomp into the kitchen

We watched Father
climb onto a chair and table,
unhook the hanging wire
and lower the bulb
Then Mother
turned off
the remaining lights
and we gathered around
under the single bulb
Flying ants swirled in a frenzy
In the water's ripples our family's eyes
sparkled inexplicably
and laughed inexplicably

Many years have passed
Like a flying ant, my father
flew into another basin
and we left our old home
For a long time, we haven't heard
the sound of clogs

My young daughter and son ask,
Was that Grandpa's idea?

人傷感了
一時便不懂得回答
也叫他們
端盤水來
請嫲嫲安坐廳中
然後，把所有的窗打開
把所有的燈熄滅

不是風雨前夕
自然不見飛蟻蓬飛
但我們倒喜歡
點一盞燈
低低垂近水面
聽嫲嫲搖着蒲扇
述說兒時光景
孩子們的眼睛
也像當年我們的眼睛
奇異地閃
奇異地笑

是許多年前的一個夜麼
是許多年後的一盤水
我們像飛蟻飛來
也會像飛蟻飛去
在燈光的下面
在燈光的上面
水紋裏我們看見
自己的眼睛
一家子快樂的眼睛
和曾經瀲灔
又永恆地瀲灔

至愛的眼睛

In my sorrow
I don't know how to respond
So I tell them to bring me
a basin of water,
invite Grandma into the sitting room
and open all the windows
and turn off all the lights

It's not the eve of a rainstorm
We won't see flying ants swirl
but we'd still like
to light a lamp,
lean in toward the water
and listen to Grandma, waving her palm-leaf fan,
recounting scenes from childhood
The children's eyes
like ours from years ago
sparkling wondrously
laughing wondrously

Is this a night from many years before?
Is this a basin from many years later?
We flew here like flying ants
and we'll fly away like flying ants
under the light
above the light
in the ripples of water where we see
our own eyes
the joyful eyes of an entire family
and the once-undulating
eternally undulating

eyes of the beloved

背痛

咳就咳吧
要命是
背後見痛
驚恐是醫生要你照肺
要命是
焦慮
燈箱上兩片肺葉
完整　又安好
咳就由它咳好了
問題是
背後見痛
一瀝復一瀝
一星期復一星期
七七四十九頭七接尾七
一日比一日見瘦
一絲一縷
感覺蠕動
纏着喉頭
纏着胸口
咳就咳吧最好咳個半死
咳至吐血痙攣呼天搶地然後
電療用刀割然後
浮過　或浮不過
生命
的海
要命是
焦慮
燈箱上

Back Pain

OK, I'll cough—
what's really killing me is
my back
Panic is when a doctor wants to see through you—
what's really killing me is
anxiety
Two lungs appear on the light box
sound   and intact
Cough, just cough it out—
the problem is
my back hurts
One spasm after another,
one week after another,
seven times seven equals forty-nine days of the dead
Each day thinner than ever
Each tiny sensation
feels like something crawling
gripping my throat
gripping my chest
Cough, just cough until I'm halfway to death
cough until I'm spitting up blood, cramping and screaming
Electrotherapy, surgery and then
floating   or drowning
in the sea
of life
What's really killing me is
anxiety
On the light box

兩片肺葉
完整　安好
又對稱
查不出　照不出　驗不到
為甚麼對這實證主義的世界我吐不出一口血來呢
咳　咳　咳
要命是咳
咳是現象
不是本質
痛　痛　痛
要命是痛
痛與不痛
不可相通

two lungs
sound   intact
and symmetrical
Nothing found   Nothing seen   Nothing diagnosed
Why can't I spit a mouthful of blood at this positivist world?
Cough   cough   cough
What's really killing me is my cough—
coughing is a phenomenon
not an essence
Pain   pain   pain
What's really killing me is pain—
pain and no-pain
will never meet

靜夜思

那些深秋的蟲聲
和砵仔糕一同消失
是打哪時開始呢
偶爾從書頁裏轉過頭來
母親的蒲扇
鬼狐的影子
像鑿壁偷光的童子
窺見星天之外
貓的眼睛
賣飛機欖那把嗓音
仍然沙啞蒼涼
劃過長長一彎
時空軌跡
像一枚彗星
曳著生澀的一綫味兒
周而復始
周而復轉
那些收買爛洋遮手錶的
彷若當年矮牆日影
給轉響手上的搖鼓迷亂了
叮咚逶迤
便都到了眼前
尾隨着
趕上鏟刀磨鉸剪
和一長串一長串
買衣裳竹的叫聲
種種聲調悠揚的生意
像描在黃草紙上的
墨跡，沁透紙背；也沁透

Quiet Night Thoughts

Those sounds of late autumn insects
have vanished along with pudding cakes
When did all this begin to happen?
Occasionally I turn from my book
Mother's palm-leaf fan
and the shadow of a ghostly fox appear
I'm like the boy who made a secret hole in his wall to get more light,
peeping beyond the starry sky
at a cat's eyes
A voice selling *Airplane olives!*
still hoarse and forlorn
arcing in long curves
a trail through time and space
like a comet
carrying a hint of bitterness
circling back for a fresh start
circling back for another cycle
Shadows from the past on a low wall,
those dealers buying damaged umbrellas and watches
muddled by a shaking tambourine
meandering in a clamor
all arriving in front of me
followed by
Knife and scissor sharpening!
and strings and strings of voices
selling bamboo poles for clothing
All sorts of melodious peddling
like sketches on thin yellow paper
with traces of ink bleeding through, bleeding through

歲月的
這一邊
如果運氣好
無關乎陰晴圓缺
街的轉角
「啲打」聲響
一挺棺木在前
行行重行行
相逢未必曾相識
石板的街衢
陡峭的斜坡
聽過算命銅鑼
和流浪的三弦琴響
隨便一歇
回頭便驚覺
多少個杏仁茶的夏夜
多少個芝麻糊的冬天
如今，我想學當年的大人
燙一壺酒
送一盅禾蟲
但縱使有弄猴的老叟經過
或燈影裏走來
推車送嫁的白洋鼠
卻那裏找得着捏麵人
將那等光怪的人和事
諸般
搓捏
何時呢我像我飄泊多年的父親
也望著悠悠月色
惘惘然對膝下的人兒
發怔
「故家的床前
有口水井……」

this side
of time
If fortune smiled
whether the moon dimmed or shone, waxed or waned
I'd turn a corner onto a street
and hear bleats from a funeral horn
with a coffin coming into view
leading mourners processing on and on
Chance encounters between those who've never met—
On a street steeply inclined
and paved with slabs of stone
I heard the fortune teller's gong
and the sound of a wandering lute
Stopping for a short rest
I looked back with a start:
so many summer nights of almond tea
so many winter days of sesame soup
Now I want to act like a grown-up from those years
warm a jug of wine
to go with a pot of worms
But even if the old showman comes by with his monkey
or white mice appear pulling a wedding carriage
out of a lantern's shadow
where can one still find the figurine man
forming bizarre characters and stories
out of rice flour, kneading them
into all kinds of shapes
When did I become like my long-wandering father
looking up at the streaming moonlight
and gazing in bewilderment
at children underfoot
Before my hometown bed
there's a well . . .

機遇

機遇到來
我得以
望着你

在山中
望着你
在水中
望着你
機遇到來我得以
望着你

望着你
我失去
好的東西
望着你
我失去
壞的東西
機遇到來
我　望着你

在山中
失去山
在水中
失去水
在在中
失去在
在你中

An Occasion

An occasion arises
and I can
look at you

Amid the mountains
looking at you
amid the waters
looking at you
An occasion arises and I can
look at you

Looking at you
I lose
the good things
looking at you
I lose
the bad things
An occasion arises
I   look at you

Amid the mountains
losing the mountains
amid the waters
losing the waters
Amid being
losing being
amid you

失去
我自己

機遇到來
我失去
垂手
可得
整個世界
望着你

望着你

失去你然而
望着你

I lose
myself

An occasion arises
and I lose
an entire world
at my
fingertips
Looking at you

Looking at you

Losing you and yet
looking at you

皇帝的新衣

皇帝穿上新衣
露出了
無形
的手

這秘密
除了那孩子
全國的男女
都知道

所以他們
如此一致
任由後世恥笑

The Emperor's New Clothes

The emperor put on his new clothes
and exposed
an invisible
hand

Except for the child
all the people
in the kingdom
knew this secret

which is why
altogether they bear
the laughter of their descendants

等待97並果陀

一滴水
滴進湖裏
的痛苦
我有
我時而是水
時而
是湖

一滴水
滴進乾涸的大地
的痛苦
我也有
時而我是
乾涸的大地
時而
我是
那水滴

但一滴水
滴進乾涸的大地
的快樂呢？

一滴水
滴進湖裏
的狂喜呢？

Waiting for '97 and Godot

The torment
of a drop of water
falling into a lake
I know—
at times I am the drop of water
at times
I am the lake

The torment
of a drop of water
falling onto the parched earth
I also know
At times I am
the parched earth
At times
I am
that droplet

But what about the joy
of a drop of water
falling onto the parched earth?

What about the ecstasy
of a drop of water
falling into the lake?

縱使
我時而是水
時而是大地
時而是江河湖泊
時而狂喜時而痛苦時而快樂
時而
我說服自己
你
終將到來

Even though
at times I am the water
at times I am the earth
at times I am the rivers and lakes
at times ecstatic at times tormented at times joyful
at times
I persuade myself
that you
will eventually arrive

蝴蝶拍翼

「人生最大的悲哀
是回頭
回絕了
又回頭
並且是
永劫
回頭。」

轉戰千里轉戰
千年
傳說中一勇武
將軍
勝利凱旋最終
回返家鄉

「你的頭呢？」
他曾經的
愛人問。
將軍頹然
警覺
該是
倒下去的時候了

你的
頭呢
刑天老先生
你的頭呢
施洗者約翰
你的
掛在很遠很遠的樹上

A Butterfly Flaps Its Wings

The greatest sorrow in life
is to turn your head,
to turn back
after turning something down,
a kind of
eternal
turn of the head.

Fighting across thousands of miles fighting
over a thousand years
a legendary, valiant
general
returned home at last
in triumph

Where's your head?
asked his
former lover
Aghast, the general
suddenly realized
that it must
be time to collapse

Where's
your head,
Old Mr. Xingtian?
Where's your head,
John the Baptist?
Where's your head—
hanging from a faraway tree,

飛翔在很近很近的雲端
你的，我的
頭呢？余麗珍娘娘

我從不照鏡
自離別出發
我從不自以為
隨時撫摸到
自己的腦袋
轉戰千年轉戰千里
我從不
叫我的武士
歸家

破釜
沉舟
過目
即忘
義無反顧我下達
禁令
禁止他們
像儒雅多情
關雲長
一顧二顧頻頻回顧
且閒時撥弄
三千丈
的鬍子

然而
當千山之外
甚麼地方一隻
受傷的蝴蝶
拍翼

soaring in a nearby cloud?
Where's yours, where's mine,
Headless Empress Yu Lai-zhen?

I never looked in mirrors
after my departure
I never assumed
I could always touch
my own skull
Fighting over a thousand years fighting across thousands of miles
I never
ordered my warriors
to return home

Sinking
our boats
Uncommitted
to memory
Honor bound not to return, I issued
a prohibition
to ban them
from gentlemanly sentiments
like General Guan Yu
who looked back once, twice, again and again
and fiddled in his free time
with his three-thousand-foot
beard

And yet
when over thousands of mountains
somewhere
an injured butterfly
flaps its wings

無原由我的武士
便會無端
激動
揮舞彩繪
的戰斧
尋找
渾忘
已久
失落
經年
自己的
以至別人的
頭顱了

你的，我的，頭呢？

愛人，這是多麼慘烈的苦刑者永劫輪迴的知覺
與記憶啊
直至不知甚麼年了
甚麼地方一隻
蝴蝶，像你
千里飛臨
閃靈般
進入
無物之物
那些苦痛的靈魂
才酣然倒地
撫摸無痕
的傷痛
夢一輩子
又一輩子
無夢
的夢

my warriors
get excited
for no reason
brandishing colorful
battle axes
searching for
what's been forgotten
for a long time
and lost
over the years:
their own heads
and even the heads
of others

Where's your head, where's mine?

My love, how traumatic this eternal return of sensations and memories
of one tortured
until a year I don't know when
somewhere
a butterfly like you
arrives from a thousand miles away
like a shining sprite
entering
objects of emptiness
and those suffering souls
happily collapse in a daze
touching their sorrows
that are missing their scars
dreaming for one lifetime
after another
a dream
of no dreams

施水大娘（母親講的故事）

背着因襲的重擔，肩着黑暗的
閘門，放他們到光明的遠處
　　　　　——魯迅

旅人跋涉長途唇焦舌燥
轉過山崖轉過山凹輾轉

烈日下終於來到
茶水茅亭
茅亭內施水大娘杓子一舀
清亮亮便注了滿滿一碗
遞給旅人又兀自
朝碗內撒下
一泡穀糠
氣喘如牛焦渴若火
旅人恨不得跳進井裏
泉裏湖裏江河裏
此刻
也得端起碗來
悠悠慢慢
將穀糠吹散
對這大娘心存感激
又納悶不解
不解她
何以好心沒有做盡
送佛只送到山崖
卻也得端起碗來

The Auntie Who Offered Water
(A Story from My Mother)

Bear the burden of old customs and shoulder the dark
gate, release our children into the bright distance
—Lu Xun

A traveler walks a long way with parched lips and a dry tongue
winding around a cliff, winding around a valley, zigzagging

Under the scorching sun he finally arrives
for refreshment at a thatched pavilion
At the pavilion an auntie scoops up a ladle
of bright, clean water and fills a bowl to the brim,
handing it to the traveler and thereupon
sprinkles into the bowl
a handful of dried rice husks
Huffing like a cow, burning with thirst
dying to jump into a well
a spring a lake a river
at this moment
the traveler can only pick up his bowl
and slowly and gently
blow away the husks
grateful for this auntie
but puzzled at the same time,
not understanding
why her good deed wasn't completed
like leaving the Buddha on a cliff halfway home
but he can only pick up his bowl

悠悠慢慢
將穀糠吹散
將水喝盡
道謝再三
趕路而去

人人若此個個如是
過路的人與路過的人
也得端起碗來，將穀糠吹散
將水喝盡，道謝再三，趕路而去
一路上他們感激茶水
卻又抱怨穀糠

如是者若干年後據說
一位風水先生趕路路過
毒日炎炎灼灼火燒
水濺石上給他忽兒
悟到：行色匆匆吹去穀糠
是緩緩的
一種紓解
待得內熱吐盡心氣平順
把水灌下才保
益壽延年
想這大娘好心若此細心若此
於是捲起衣衫指點江山
指點給她
千金難得曠世難求
一處
龍口地
果真福有攸歸風水隨人
及後大娘老去安葬其中
子孫於是興發

and slowly and gently
blow away the husks
guzzling all the water,
thanking her again and again
and hurrying off

Everyone, everyone is like this
Passersby and people passing by
can only pick up their bowls and blow away the husks,
guzzling the water, giving thanks again and again and hurrying off
Along the way they're grateful for a drink
but complain about the husks

And so it was until some years later it was said
that a feng-shui master had passed by—
on a poisonously scorching and sizzling day
water splashed on a stone and suddenly
he had a vision: hurrying on a journey and blowing away the husks
eases us into
a kind of relief
Only when our internal heat releases and the mind calms
can the water pouring down our throat be sure
to lengthen our life
Thinking of the auntie's kindness and attentiveness
he rolled up his sleeves and surveyed the horizon,
pointing her
to a spot
that's one in a million, once in a lifetime,
a land equal to a dragon's treasure
Truly fortune favors the good and feng-shui follows the blessed
The auntie was buried there after her death
And so her family blossomed

家宅於是榮華
這「墳」的故事於是流傳至今
人人樂道津津……只是

只是會稽魯迅
對這天理循環
照例報以呵呵一笑……但
看官且看
他也從此橫起眉頭
不但挶住黑暗的閘門
且硬要派給
那些跨向光明的過客
每人一副「ＸＸ」太陽眼鏡

and her descendants prospered
This "grave" story has been passed down to this day
Everyone loves to talk about it—except

except for Lu Xun from Kuaiji
who laughed as usual at the idea
that "what goes around comes around" . . . but
dear onlookers, please observe
that henceforth he scowled
and not only held open the gate of darkness
but insisted on giving
each passerby who stepped toward the brightness
a pair of _____ sunglasses

巴士驟停

巴士驟停
我一頭撞在窗玻璃上
所以你上車時沒看見我
你只見
巴士驟停
一個人
的頭飛出車窗
你只見
玻璃迸碎
巴士
驟停

「這就是
你受傷的地方麼？」
握着你伸來
探問的手
我望着前面
驟停
的巴士
遙想
上車的乘客
是你
而我是
車上
那毛躁小子
奇蹟
前來
卻驟然
昏厥

The Braking Bus

The bus stopped suddenly
My head crashed through the windowpane
so you didn't see me when you got on
You only saw
the bus stop suddenly
and someone's head
fly out the window
You only saw
glass shattering
The bus
stopping suddenly

Is this
where you were injured?
I held your hand
reaching out to me
I looked at the bus ahead
stopping suddenly
in front of us
I imagined
you were the passenger
getting on
and I was
that rash boy
on the bus
A miracle
approaching
as I
blacked out

「對誰
這有好處呢？」
你一路上奔走嗚咽
彷彿你從沒有踏上那巴士
我也從沒有從那座椅上遽然站起
彷彿那巴士沒有驟然停住
而我狂喜的頭顱
也沒有穿越玻璃
重又接回
吾的軀體

這所謂
的遭逢
該如何說起？

還是漸長的女兒
最是墮入情節
「老爹
你們是怎樣相識的呢
你們
那個
所謂
的你們
究竟
終究
有沒有
（喂）
相識呢？」

What good
does this do anyone?
You whimpered while you ran
as if you'd never set foot on the bus
and I'd never stood up abruptly from my seat
as if the bus had not stopped suddenly
and my head enraptured
had not passed through the glass
reconnecting
again with my body

How should we describe
this so-called
"encounter"

In the end my growing daughter
is the one most invested in the plot:
Pops,
how did you two meet?
Did you two
or those
so-called
"you two"
after all
at last
ever
(hey!)
meet each other?

蛇王詩抄 (選四)

（一）讀詩

我們的詩是押在褲頭讀的
掏出來和塞回去
都得左顧右盼

（二）趕巴士

趕搭冇蓋巴士
它載我們
到遠方避雨

（三）安全守則

安全守則貼在牆上
對照着我們檢查自己
檢查守則，然後
檢查各自的運氣

（四）仰望

艙底究竟多深
大伙兒都不知道
累極了我們便仰望
但從不丈量　　天堂

Collected Poems from the King of Laziness (4 Selections)

1. Reading Poems

We tuck our poems inside our waistbands to read them
pulling them out and stuffing them back in
glancing sideways all the while

2. Chasing a Bus

Chasing a bus without a rooftop
It carries us
toward a distant shelter from the rain

3. Safety Guidelines

Safety guidelines on the wall—
mirroring them, we check ourselves,
check the guidelines, and then,
we each check our own luck

4. Looking Up

How deep is the ship's cabin?
None of us knows the answer
Exhausted we look up
but never fathom   heaven

驚髮

理髮店的旋轉標誌
旋轉得越來越急速
有的橫放，打破規格
有的變作圓環，多了些顏色
從前剪了髮才洗頭
現在次序顛倒
母親硬要我們的頭
剪得光脫脫的
那時我們哭喪着臉
她卻朝鏡子裏笑
軟綿綿的毛絨球
香撲鼻的爽身粉
連環圖一本本霸在膝上
一頁頁如風吹揭
理髮椅的扶手
橫架一塊木板
坐在上面挺威風的
我們又每每惱怨
想望一天
隨手可把它扔掉……
鏡子前後，人來人往
鏡子裏外
春花秋月
嬗變的髮式
一次比一次趨時
攬鏡自照
一次比一次
更鍾愛自己

Startling Hair

The swirling poles of the barber shops
swirl at greater and greater speed
Some lie horizontally now, smashing the norm
Some have become rings with added colors
They used to wash our hair after cutting it
Now the order's reversed
Mother had insisted on our heads
being shaved bare—
She smiles in the mirror
at our faces in tears
Sweet-smelling talcum powder
from a feathery brush
Comic books commandeered on laps
Pages flipping as if blown by the wind
Across the arms of the barber's chair
rests a wooden board
We sit up straight with pride
though sometimes we grumble
hoping for a day
when it can be cast aside
Before and behind the mirror people come and go
Within and beyond the mirror
spring flowers bloom and the autumn moon wanes
Hairstyles evolve
each one timelier than the last
Holding up a mirror
I admire myself more
and more each time

直到一天
脖子上抖落未盡
細碎的髮屑我們驚覺
鏡裏眾多容顏
獨不見母親
猛然轉過頭來
慌亂中幸好
見母親剛從巷口走進
且帶來輕軟茸茸
毛絨球的感覺
和爽身粉般
香撲鼻的記憶
雖則，她的鬢髮一夜白了
而我們兄弟多人
近日少從鏡裏回望
所以一無所知
彷彿一無所知

until one day
shaking the endless hair clippings
from our necks, we're startled
by the absence of Mother's face
in a mirror full of faces
I turn around abruptly
in a panic, but fortunately
I see Mother just walking in from the alley
bringing the soft, light
feeling of a barber's brush
and the sweet-smelling memories
of talcum powder
even though her hair turned white overnight
and we brothers
don't look in the mirror much anymore
so that's why we know nothing
why it seems we know nothing

寬容者

一隻蟑螂爬行我眼前

一隻蟑螂。不期然我攤開我的手掌並高高舉放半空。

蟑螂緩緩爬行。牠緩緩爬行又停在我眼前的書頁上。

牠的觸鬚擺弄。而我的手掌停放半空凝定在牠擺弄着的觸鬚之上。

我看着我的手掌。那蟑螂也是。牠也看着正置於牠頭上的我的手掌。

我的手掌張開。我的手掌張開這使牠清楚看到我此刻一無所持。沒通常的拿着一隻拖鞋。沒拿着捲成長條的舊報紙。沒拿着講稿草稿詩論稿各種開度的白皮書綠皮書報告書。甚至沒戴上一拍即丟各款不同顏色與質料的手套。這，使我很尷尬。這是自然而然攤開手掌發覺一無所持的尷尬。

牠看了看我一無所持的手掌。又緩緩爬行。牠緩緩爬過我眼前潔淨的書頁。觸鬚擺弄倨傲的神情。不知是對書頁上的文字輕蔑還是對我此刻凝定的姿態輕蔑。牠緩緩爬行。從桌子的一邊爬行到桌子的另一邊。從一組文字爬過另一組文字。時間悠長。時間悠長足夠我舉起手掌又停放半空在今後悠長的一生裏思索「寬容」。和寬容者攤開手掌而發覺一無所持的尷尬。與沮喪。

A Tolerant Person

A cockroach crawls in front of me

A cockroach. Without thinking I spread my palm and lift it high in the air.

The cockroach crawls slowly. It crawls slowly and stops on the page in front of me.

Its antennae fidget. And my palm stays still in the air above its fidgeting antennae.

I look at my palm. The cockroach, too. It, too, looks at my palm held above its head.

My palm opens. My palm opens, making it clear to the cockroach that I am not depending on anything now. Not on the slipper that I usually hold. Not on an old, rolled-up newspaper. Not on the draft of a speech, not on the draft of poetry criticism, no drafts of any kind, no white paper no green paper no other paper of any size. Not even disposable gloves of various colors and kinds. This—it makes me embarrassed. It is the embarrassment of spreading one's naked palm without thinking and realizing one has nothing to rely on.

The cockroach looks at my naked palm that relies on nothing. Crawling slowly again. It crawls along the clean pages in front of me. Its antennae fidget arrogantly. I don't know if its contempt is for the words on the page or for my frozen gesture. It crawls slowly. Crawling from one side of the table to the other. From one group of words to another. Time stretches. Time long enough for me to raise my palm and hold it in the air and think about "tolerance" over the length of a lifetime—and the embarrassment and dismay of a tolerant person who opens his naked palm and finds it relies on nothing.

煙花練習 (二十)

一枚海螺
黑夜裏
吹響彩色的歌

一株珊瑚
異鄉的魚
游來游往

金髮妖女
從古瓶走出
搖動着魔鏡

頑皮仙子
恣意拋擲
幸福的玻璃

無數荊棘
招引無數荊鳥
深夜啼血

迷途天使
繞着夢中之樹
焚燒落英

命運的女神
拋散紙牌
赴約而去

Exercises in Fireworks (20)

On a dark night
a single conch
blows particolored songs

Fish from another sea
crisscross
a branch of coral

A blond enchantress
emerges from an antique bottle
waving a magical mirror

A mischievous sprite
tosses around
blessed pieces of glass

At night countless thorns
entice countless thorn birds
to cry out until they bleed

An angel astray
encircles a make-believe tree
burning its fallen petals

The goddess of fate
flings away her tarot cards
sweeping off to an appointment

眾生的輪
輪迴轉動
世世代代的奇蹟

永恆的水晶球
耐不住永恆貞潔
倏忽迸碎

古典的油紙傘
遮擋不絕
浪漫的流星

那是金蛇狂舞
爭一面明鏡

那是翻江蛟龍
臨崖濺血

那是汗血天馬
大漠奔星

那是英雄聚義
擊掌歃血

那是一枝迷迭香
開在幻象之谷

那是漫天螢火蟲
歡度潑水節

那是夜貓的眼裏
幽玄的淚滴

The wheel of life
reincarnating and generating
generations of miracles

An eternal crystal ball
cannot bear its eternal chastity
and explodes all at once

An oil-paper parasol
protects against endless,
romantic shooting stars

That's the mad dance of the golden snake
outshining a bright mirror

That's the river-flipping water dragon
gushing blood on a cliff

That's the blood-sweating horse from heaven
chasing stars in the desert

That's a gathering of heroic warriors
striking each other's palms with blood oaths

That's a sprig of rosemary
blooming in the valley of delusions

That's a sky thick with fireflies
spraying water in new-year celebration

That's a mysterious teardrop
welling in a night cat's eye

那是遠古女奴
圖解宮廷光景

那是思鄉的吳剛
搖落繽紛桂子

那是寂寞的嫦娥
吹散惱人的蒲公英

That's an ancient female slave
depicted in a palace scene

That's Wu Gang homesick on the moon
shaking loose the osmanthus drupes

That's the lunar goddess Chang'e
blowing on a bothersome dandelion

我有面頰

我有面頰
但求一吻
我有嘴唇
但求可吻

但任我的面頰
如何遷就
任我的嘴唇
如何追索

任轉動的頭
如何飛快
任它們本來
如何接近

I Have Cheeks

I have cheeks
just needing a kiss
I have lips
just needing to kiss

But no matter how
my cheeks oblige
No matter how
my lips persist

No matter how fast
my head spins round
no matter how close
they are to each other

報告書123

1： 七十歲就那麼老
　　造成改革的障礙

2： 六歲至六十九歲（註）
　　又那麼亢奮
　　沒甚麼力量
　　可以抗衡

3： 新生的一代
　　情況可能好轉
　　狼頒佈律例
　　羊不再吃人

註：「因為教育，野心從六歲開始。」
1968年法國學生運動牆頭標語。佚名。

Report 123

1: One's already old by the age of seventy
   causing an impediment to reform

2: While ages six to sixty-nine*
   are too excitable
   to have the strength
   to oppose anyone

3: A new generation
   may improve the situation
   The wolves issue a law:
   sheep can no longer eat people

*"Because of education, ambition begins at the age of six."
Slogan written on a wall during the 1968 student movement
in France. Anonymous.

啞願

死因聆訊
因為我
中途缺席
你被剝奪
發言的權利
戰爭再一次
血腥地
被無望
的和平
打斷
我曾目睹
暮色蒼茫
的界碑
抹去又重寫的
墓誌銘
這是關乎萬民的訊息
但我回來
只是聆聽
再不會宣說

Mute Wish

A hearing on the cause of death—
since I absented myself
halfway through
you were deprived
of the right to speak
Once again war was
bloodily
interrupted
by a hopeless
peace
I have witnessed
a boundary stone
in the twilight hour,
its epitaph
erased and rewritten
It was a message concerning all people
Yet I will return
only to listen
and proclaim nothing

盲流

終點是盲目；我出發前便已達到。

我盲
故我流

流向西流向東流向南流向北
流向未來
的震撼
流向原始
的歸復

我盲
故我流

流向紅流向橙流向青流向黃流向綠
流向藍流向紫
流向彩虹
之上
流向黑洞
之中

我盲，故我流
流向1流向2流向3流向4流向5流向6
流向既定
的秩序
流向非既定
的約束

Blind Drifting

My destination was blindness; I arrived before setting off.

I am blind
therefore I drift

Drift toward the west drift toward the east drift toward the south
    drift toward the north
Drift toward the shock
of the future
Drift toward the return
of the origin

I am blind
therefore I drift

Drift toward red drift toward orange drift toward indigo
    drift toward yellow drift toward green
Drift toward blue drift toward violet
Drift above
a rainbow
Drift inside
a black hole

I am blind, therefore I drift
Drift toward 1 drift toward 2 drift toward 3 drift toward 4
    drift toward 5 drift toward 6
Drift toward
established order
Drift toward
unestablished constraints

我盲，故我流

流向A流向B
流向ABCDZE
流向適當
的傾斜
流向更適當
的傾覆

我盲，故我流

流向左流向右流向前流向後
流向無私無我無往而不義
的大道
流向無原無由無所不向其極
的迷宮

我盲，故我流
流向超前　的陷阱
流向滯後　的深谷

流向聲光建構
流向紋飾符籙
流向名與利的關口
流向權和力的裂縫
流向解體建造釋放牢籠
流向規整喜樂越軌悲哭

我盲，故我流
流向迴環流向往復
流向實有流向虛空
流向表裏澄澈

I am blind, therefore I drift

Drift toward A drift toward B
Drift toward ABCDZE
Drift toward a suitable
tilting
Drift toward a more suitable
toppling

I am blind, therefore I drift

Drift toward the left drift toward the right drift toward
    the front drift toward the back
Drift toward the boulevard
of no-self no-ego no-unrighteousness
Drift toward the maze
of no origin no reason no endpoint without its extremity

I am blind, therefore I drift
Drift toward the advancing   snare
Drift toward the lagging   ravine

Drift toward the structure of sound and light
Drift toward ornamentations and talismanic scripts
Drift toward the gateway of fame and fortune
Drift toward the cracks in authority and power
Drift toward disintegrating constructions and liberating prisons
Drift toward orderly joy and deviant sorrow

I am blind, therefore I drift
Drift toward circularity drift toward seesawing
Drift toward solidity drift toward the void
Drift toward outward and inward clarity

流向彎曲復彎曲
流向筆直又筆直
流向鏡像之無窮

流向虛無
和對虛無的批判
流向批判　又批判的批判
的運動　運動　運動

我盲，故我流
流向速朽流向圓熟流向躁動流向靜穆
流向冷熱交煎的陣痛
流向絕望又希望之母腹

流向天國車站
流向地獄之門

流向給定的
罪與罰
流向應許的夢應許的救贖應許的樂土
應許者應許
的懷抱

我盲，故我流
流向歷史的必然
之惡
流向無可無不可
的血淚之中

Drift toward recurring curves
Drift toward the straightening after straightening
Drift toward the infinity of mirrored images

Drift toward nothingness
and the critique of nothingness
Drift toward the movement   movement   movement of
critique   and the critique of critique

I am blind, therefore I drift
Drift toward rapid decay drift toward aptitude drift toward
    agitation drift toward solemnity
Drift toward the alternating chill and heat of labor pains
Drift toward the womb of despair and hope

Drift toward heaven's station
Drift toward the gates of hell

Drift toward the appointed
crime and punishment
Drift toward the promised dream the promised redemption
    the promised land
The promiser's
promised embrace

I am blind, therefore I drift
Drift toward the inevitable evil
of history
Drift toward noncommittal
blood and tears

流向金色銀色的檔案
流向紅色黑色的
備忘錄

我盲，故我流

流向中心四散
流向金木水火土
流向宇宙大爆炸
流向熱的第二定律

流向悲劇的誕生
流向命運的播弄
流向獅身人像的迷
流向魔女羅累萊的歌哭
流向預先張揚的一樁命案
流向陰差陽錯設定的佈局

流向難以忍受的輕
流向難以忍受的重
流向更難以忍受的
眾神之默默
眾人之　掌聲雷動

我流，故我盲

流向與生俱來一個情結
流向天造地設一大報復
流向哀痛莫名
我剜掉雙眼時
光明與黑暗
之一瞬

Drift toward the golden the silver archives
Drift toward the red the black
memoranda

I am blind, therefore I drift

Drift toward the scattering center
Drift toward the five elements
Drift toward the Big Bang
Drift toward the second law of thermodynamics

Drift toward the birth of tragedy
Drift toward the tinkering of fate
Drift toward the riddle of the Sphinx
Drift toward the wailing song of the siren Lorelei
Drift toward a death foretold
Drift toward a composition arranged by mishaps

Drift toward the unbearable lightness
Drift toward the unbearable heaviness
Drift toward the even more unbearable
silence of the gods
the thunderous applause   of the people

I drift, therefore I am blind

Drifting toward an innate obsession
Drifting toward unbearable lightness, the perfectly matched
    grand reprisal
Drifting toward indescribable anguish
in that instant
of radiance and darkness
when I gouge out my eyes

冥想曲

給阿悅

她／他說：「你地摸我啦，你
地摸我，就知道我點解鍾意愛
鍾意和平，唔鍾意戰爭。」

本來無一物
原來　我是我自己的塵埃

泰綺思　　唯你沉淪　　曾經是
眾生的拯救

在粵語殘境中遇見你
那天　琴聲如訴

我在你素淨的默想中
把弄聖言　開口卻是蝴蝶

而你朝聞道
我　倏忽已老

多少人愛你聖潔的面容　光輝
從前　銷魂結舌　一一被你取悅

唯我輪迴　思想你當日的形影
乜水之南　乜水之東

乜水之西　乜水之北

Méditation

For Ah Yu

S/he said, "Come here and caress me—ah, if you all
caress me, you'll know why I like love
and peace and not war."

In the beginning there was nothing
It turned out   I was my own dust

Thaïs   you alone in ruin   once
saved the living

I came upon you in an old Cantonese movie
That day   its music cried out to me

Amid your quiet meditations
I dabbled in holy words   yet butterflies emerged from my mouth

and when you learned about the Way in the morning
I suddenly   became old

So many men fell in love with your divine face   your radiance
They were once   speechless and lost in ecstasy   pleased one by one

I alone reincarnated   imagining silhouettes of you from the past
south of a nameless river   east of a nameless river

west of a nameless river   north of a nameless river

搬石

我喜歡
終有一死
那人知覺
只能如此
卻來取悅我

他取悅我
老早知悉
我創造一塊
人們搬不動
我也搬不動
的巨石

那個俗世
十足十的傻瓜
伸出手來
天真又爛漫
虛空中舞踏

「主啊，我的力量
你所賜予
讓我隨同
搬動那塊
搬不動
的巨石吧！」

Moving a Stone

I like that
death awaits everyone
and when that fellow understands
it must be so
he still tries to please me

He tries to please me
well aware
that I created
a giant stone
no one can move
including me

In his earthly realm
that perfect fool
stretches out his hands
with a bright-eyed innocence,
prancing in the void

O Lord, my strength
comes from you
Let me join you
in moving that
unmovable
giant stone!

我探出頭來
輕聲細語
「世人都禮拜
搬來搬去的巨石
你怎麼偏執
徒然往返」

他說主啊主啊
這不就是
你的大智慧麼
正因其不可能
我才相信

所以我說我喜歡
終有一死那人
知覺只能如此
卻來取悅我

噢！只能如此
恆久忍耐
誰也搬不動
終是信望愛

I poke my head out
and whisper to him,
Everybody worships
giant stones that can be moved here and there
so why insist on moving
something in vain?

He says, *O Lord, O Lord,*
isn't this
your great wisdom?
Precisely because it's impossible
I believe

That's why I said I like
that death awaits everyone and that fellow
understands it has to be like this
and yet he still tries to please me

Oh, it has to be like this
Everlasting patience:
no one can move
faith hope and love

行為藝術

給媚

丹麥美人魚尋回失頭
又是我們郁手的時候

我們以生命
的虛無
成就她
永恆
的變奏

直至我們
也成為
銅像
或石頭
塗鴉者被塗鴉
在虛擬
的牆上
哭泣
的網上
像海妖
歌唱

像海妖
靜默時
那七種
歌唱

Performance Art

for Mei

The Danish mermaid's missing head has been found
It's time for us to act again

We use life's
emptiness
to fulfill
her eternal
variations

until we too
become
a bronze statue
or a stone,
until a graffiti artist is graffitied
upon a virtual
wall,
a weeping
web that sings
like the Sirens

like the Sirens
in a time of silence
with those seven kinds
of singing

歌唱不被理解
的哀傷
和理解
尾隨

之遺忘

sung with the sorrow
of not being understood
and of the forgetfulness
that follows

understanding

一個入處／休歇處

母親挨近床沿
船便起航了
有人匆匆才趕至
跨過甲板
擠入人堆中
要想覓得
一個休歇處

「鄉親父老且讓讓
我來講故事」

我們蜷曲挨擠
母親直直坐在床邊
抑揚婉轉
就那麼一句

「深山有隻老禾雀——」

船上那人見放得下行李
趁勢便坐在旁邊
抬頭朝好奇的眼睛一抹
一轉，像吐露又掩藏
一大秘密

「毛都冇條架……」

大家聽見越發驚怪
慌忙退讓出更大空間
卻見那人打過呵欠

An Entryway / A Resting Place

Mother leaned toward the edge of the bed
and the boat began to set sail
Someone rushed aboard just in time
stepping across the deck
squeezing into the crowd
trying to find
a resting place

My dear folks, make way
and let me tell a story

We curled up and huddled against each other
Mother sat up straight in bed
and in a melodic voice
spoke just one sentence:

Deep in the mountains, there was an old sparrow—

The man on board saw that he could put his luggage down
and seized his chance to sit
Lifting his head toward puzzled eyes, he glanced around
and squinted, appearing ready to divulge and to hide
a great secret

with not a single pube . . .

More and more surprised, everyone
scrambled to back up and make space
but then the man began to yawn

把腿兒舒伸
矇頭便睡去了

我們聽得興起
自然要跟著起哄
但見母親把紙扇收合
輕輕朝我們眉心一點

「傻仔，毛都冇條
又點有尾！」

傾聽者如夢
卻醒，世界閃現
又退隱
才打開那麼一綫
柳暗花明原來
別有一番
遮掩
欸乃一聲
母親一搖
一搧
萬物於焉
浮湧
我們晃蕩
如船，跌宕
如船，在無有終始

那水域

現在看山是山
或者，看水
不再是水

stretch his legs
and fall right asleep

We were just getting interested
so naturally we egged Mother on
but she only closed her paper fan,
tapping it gently between our eyebrows

*If there's not a single pube, silly boys,
how could there be a 'tale?'*

The listeners awoke
as if from a dream, the world flashed by
and then drew back
opening a seam
into dense willows and bright flowers,
only to become another kind of
concealment
Like the creak of an oar
Mother snapped
and waved her fan
The world of ten thousand things
swelled to the surface
as we swayed
like a boat, bobbing
like a boat, in waters without

a beginning or an end

You see mountains
as mountains or water
as no longer water

擾攘人世比當日
那船艙
還擠迫
蜷曲着身體／靈魂
你總歸常常憶念
那麼一些
年月
那麼一些
故事

妙不可言，當天
母親把紙扇關收
隨手在我們眉心
一點，你發覺
或者，許多年後
你才發覺
那便是
夢
的
一個

入處

也是夢
（如果有）
的一個
休歇處

噢，船開了
天下最傻最傻的人兒
且讓讓
母親講故事……

In a bustling world
even more crowded
than the boat's cabin the other day
you curl up your body / soul
always missing
such times
as those
such stories
as those

More amazing than words: on that day
Mother closed her paper fan,
casually tapping it between
our eyebrows, you realized
or only many years later
did you realize
that it was
an
entryway
into

a dream

and a
resting place
of a dream
(if there was one)

Oh, the ship is casting off
Make way
silliest child of all
Let Mother tell her story—

第三岸

維根斯坦寫詩
我們準備玻璃
當語言穿過

當維特根斯坦穿過
當維特特根斯坦攜同他的語言穿過
就有光
彎曲
折斷
        偏移
在不可言說的
雪上

無有硬度
無有色彩
無有　甚至　所謂
覆蓋

只有死者生前
對生者死後的懷想
在河的第一岸

在河的第二岸

只有生者生前對死者死後的懷想

The Third Bank

Wittgenstein wrote a poem
We prepare glass
when language passes through

When Wittgenstine passes through
When Wittgenstinestine and his language pass through
there's a light
curving
and breaking
           sidestepping
into unspeakable
snow

without hardness
without color
without   even   a so-called
blanketing

Only the longing a dead person had while alive
for a living person after death
lies on the first bank of the river

On the second bank of the river

lies only the longing a living person while alive has for a dead person
    after death

多虧……
　　　　因為……
　　　　　　然而……
　　　　　　　　儘管……

傾拎　　筐躪

在河的
第三岸

As a result . . .

            Because . . .

                       Although . . .

                                  Despite . . .

Clinking   and clanking

on the third
bank of the river

七段狐言

「感君一回顧
風雪夜歸人」

（一）
她出現他門口
像一尾妖狐
並且不無幽怨
說：「男人
我被你追趕得好苦」

（二）
一燈如豆
一塵不染
一絲不掛
燈下她展讀
他未完成
的詩稿
忽兒轉過頭來
幽幽言說：
「這是遠古
儀式
比詩
的出現
還早呢」

A Fox's Tale in Seven Parts

Touched by your glance back,
returning home in evening snow

1.
She appeared in his doorway
like an enchanted fox
and not without resentment
said, *Mister,*
your pursuit has caused me much suffering

2.
A seed of light
A spotless room
A night undressed
Under the lamp, she unrolled and read
an unfinished
draft of his poems
At once she turned her head
and murmured,
This ancient
rite
existed
even before
poetry

（三）
趁着月色
她除下頭來
對鏡梳理
夢醒醒來
他看見了

「你怎不尖叫？」
她愣愣的，問

「是你的頭
又不是我的頭」
愣愣的，他答

（四）
媚笑着
她把他的頭
除下
雙雙對對
攬在手裏

「還笑呢，你！」
她的頭
比他的
還驚詫

「我就喜歡
這麼個樣子
我的頭
貼在你手裏」

3.
Aided by moonlight
she removed her head,
combing it in front of a mirror
Awakened from a dream
he saw her

Why didn't you scream?
she asked absently

It's your head,
not my head,
he replied absently

4.
With an enchanting smile,
she grabbed his head
and removed it,
embracing their pair of heads
with her hands

You're still smiling!
Her head
looked more surprised
than his head

I just really
like the way
my head
fits snug in your hand

（五）
回返夢裏
她將他的頭
跟她的頭
換轉
又側過臉來
調笑着說：
「可抱怨沒有
男人」

「沒有」
悠悠醒寐
他也調笑着
回答：

「我還是我的頭
且得着
你的身子呢！」

（六）
天麻麻亮了
她哭起來
「時限到了
怎生捨得離去？」

「離去吧」他說：
「就這麼個樣子
離去吧
你的一半
留在我這裏
我的一半

5.
Back inside the dream
she exchanged
his head
with her head
and leaned her face against his,
teasing,
Any complaints now,
Mister?

No
Half asleep and half awake,
he replied
teasingly,

My head's still mine
and I'm gaining
your body!

6.
As the sky dawned
she began to cry,
Our time is over
but how can I leave you?

Just go, he said,
Just go
as you are
Your half
will remain with me,
my half

跟定你
生生世世
到天涯」

（七）
踏出柴扉
她戀戀回轉頭來
「這不苦了你嗎？
男人」

「怎跟你說好呢
吾愛
這是潛藏久遠
的想望
比狐
當年逾犯天條
那夜
還早呢」

他沉沉別轉頭去
一步一步
回返夢裏

will follow you
for eternity
to the ends of the earth

7.
Stepping out of the wooden door
she turned her head with longing,
Won't this cause you suffering,
Mister?

How should I put it,
my love?
This was a long-buried
wish
well before
that night
when the foxes
violated the rules of heaven

He turned his head heavily
and step by step
returned to the dream

Somewhere . . .

東岸書店見智海畫作The Promenade有感

你相信死後得救
我相信死後自由

你相信死後得救
你是你家國的槍手
我相信死後自由
我是我自己的石頭

生活在別處
somewhere, somehow
奧斯維辛之前
奧斯維辛之後

我望你一眼
你對我微笑
（多麼容易，美好）
槍管向上
石頭大海漂浮

若不在生前
定必在死後
我不認識的你
你不認識的我

或者從不相遇
但，這已足夠

Somewhere . . .

Upon Seeing Chihoi's Series The Promenade
at the East Bank Bookstore

You believe after death lies elevation
I believe death is a liberation

You believe after death lies elevation
You are your nation's gunman
I believe death is a liberation
I am my own slingstone

Living elsewhere
somewhere, somehow
before Auschwitz
after Auschwitz

I glance at you
You smile at me
(how easily, how beautifully)
A gun barrel points skyward
A slingstone floats in the sea

If it's not before death
it must be after life
The you whom I didn't know
the you who didn't know me

may never meet
but—it will do

現成物（尿兜）

給阿石

我抱起我兒子尿尿
我想發明尿兜那人多偉大
我想我的兒子長高了
定會懷念
那尿兜
那抱抱
那尿尿

抱抱
尿尿

他此刻
俯看自己
的鳥鳥
尿尿
激射
噴濺
尿兜中
尿尿
旋轉
旋沒
他當然不會想到
長高了甚麼甚麼的
所謂
懷念

Found Object (Urinal)

For Ah Shek

I lift up my son to pee-pee
I think: how great is the person who invented the urinal
I think: when my son gets taller
he'll miss
that urinal
that lifting
that peeing

Lift me up
to pee-pee

For now he
looks down
at his wee-wee's
pee-pee
shooting
splashing
into the urinal
Pee-pee
swirling
whirling
He doesn't foresee, of course,
growing up
and so-called
reminiscing

除非
他把自己
也當作
現成物
被抱着
的雕塑
一座從遙遠遙遠
的將來
俯看
自己
鳥鳥
尿尿

的噴泉

unless
he regards himself
as a found object
being
lifted up,
a sculpture from
a faraway
future
where he looks down
at his own
wee-wee
peeing

as a fountain

掩耳盜鈴

你問我那個鈴如何被盜去
說來話長卻又簡單
那天他來到我們村裏
跟大家說起掩耳盜鈴
這故事，多荒謬可笑
大家笑彎了腰笑破肚皮
笑聲中又好像
忽然對人世間
那些愚蠢的人
平添一份尊敬
話說那人
說話又特別動聽
一遍一遍
一千遍一千遍直至
一天
我們老遠看見他
都掩住耳朵
慌忙跑開了

我們村裏那個鈴呀
它曾發出無比宏大的聲音
就在那人張開嘴巴
由遠及近
之際
光天化日
叮叮噹噹
被盜走了

Plugging Your Ears to Steal a Bell

You asked me how the bell was stolen
Well, it's a long but simple story:
One day a man came to our village
and told us about a thief who plugged his ears to steal a bell—
what a ridiculous tale!
We doubled up laughing, bursting our sides
Amid the sounds of laughter
we suddenly seemed
to have a kind of respect
for the stupid people in this world
It was said the man
was an especially moving speaker, telling his story
over and over
thousands and thousands of times until
one day
we saw him from afar
and covered our ears in fright
hurrying away

Ah, the bell in our village
It used to make an incomparable sound
Right when that man opened his mouth
and came closer and closer
right then
in broad daylight
ding-a-ling ding-a-ling
it was stolen

是呀
這就是滑稽
這就是荒謬
透頂，這就是此刻我
和你，死死把耳朵
掩住
那怕再一條村
一個鈴
一組組編鐘
一塊塊石磬
一車一船
金甌銅頭豬狗疊着
彝鼎

那怕這一切
的一切
噹噹遠逸

也不相信
也不去再聽一遍
的故事

的解釋

Oh yes
It's funny
It's ridiculous
utterly so, and that's why you
and I are dead set on plugging
our ears now
even if in another village
there's another bell
strands of chimes
slabs of stone gongs
a cart a boat
with golden chalices and copper-headed pigs and dogs stacked up
on bronze cauldrons

even if every bit
of everything
disappears with a clang

I won't believe it
and I won't
listen again

to such a tale

企放石桌

當一眾朝臣都說發現新大陸輕而易舉小事一樁，哥倫布隨手把桌上雞蛋放在大家面前，問在座誰能把雞蛋直立？眾朝臣百般把弄嘗試，都失敗。哥倫布把雞蛋拿過來，輕輕將一端敲破，便把雞蛋企立放在桌上。大家尷尬不已。只有博覽群書的皇帝暗自竊笑。他晚上才從博爾赫斯《美洲述事》那抄本中，知道當日哥倫布跟酋長打賭，眼光光看着土人將雞蛋輕敲企放石桌。但既然命運教他最終贏得美洲，所以皇帝也拍起掌來。博爾赫斯寫到皇帝暗自竊笑一段，有點忘乎所以，禁不住更安排了書中酋長土人們也隨同拍起掌來。這就是當時皇帝忽然聽到聲響，望出窗外也有一點兒尷尬不好意思的原因。

Standing an Egg on a Stone Table

When the courtiers said that discovering the New World was no great feat, Columbus grabbed an egg from the table, placed it in front of everyone, and asked who could stand the egg upright. The courtiers tried in a hundred different ways but failed. Columbus took the egg and gently cracked one end to stand it up. Everyone felt embarrassed. Only the learned king snickered to himself. The night before, he had read in a handwritten copy of Borges's *Narratives of the Americas* that Columbus once lost a bet with a chieftain and was left staring wide-eyed at the natives as they lightly cracked the end of an egg and stood it on a stone table. But since fate had ultimately delivered America into his hands, the king also began to applaud. When Borges wrote that the king snickered to himself, he got carried away and couldn't help but make the chieftain and natives in his book clap their hands, too. This is why the king, when he suddenly heard a sound and looked out the window, was also a little embarrassed.

你來就是

我思
故我是
道

路

你來
就是

你來
清掃
就是

你來
拉直它
就是

你來打個結
未嘗不可以

Just Come Along

I think
therefore I am
the way

the road

Just come
along

Just come
along
to sweep up

Just come
along
to pull it straight

Why don't you come
to make a knot?

把豉汁抹在鱠魚的身上

魚說
「你蒸我
你煎我
你翻我

為甚麼把豉汁
那麼溫柔抹在我身上」

「我憐憫自己
懸想他朝
與君體相同」

「這是人的說話麼
這是魚的說話」

「是的
當魚說話
人應該沉默

讓我把豉汁
加些許蒙汗藥
輕柔地抹在你的
我的身上」

Rubbing Black Bean Sauce on a Pomfret

A fish said,
"If you're going to steam me
and fry me
and flip me

why rub black bean sauce
on me so gently?"

"I pity myself,
envisioning one day
what you are, I will become"

"Is that a person talking?
This is a fish talking"

"Indeed
when a fish speaks
people should fall silent

Let me rub black bean sauce
and a love potion
gently on your body
and mine"

蘋果掉落和只是一首民歌

給同學政恆

（一）
蘋果從樹上掉下來的時候
牛頓抬頭剛巧看見
看見蘋果從頭頂掉下牛頓想
我看着蘋果從我頭頂掉下我能思想些甚麼呢
一任蘋果從我的頭頂掉下而已
他有點兒沮喪把頭垂下
這時恰巧上帝經過
上帝經過看見蘋果從樹上掉下
上帝發現蘋果掉下那落勢是好的
而且美麗
彷彿頭一次才看到自己的設計
和創造
無名一種感動祂要為自己的奧秘命名
於是上帝微笑着伸出祂那不無惡作劇的
可愛的小（？）手
輕輕敲了一下牛頓的腦殼
而那個差點兒掉到牛頓頭上的蘋果
上帝把它接住又滾動在牛頓若有所悟的跟前
之後眾所周知的故事
一個又一個定律發現被發現
人們過着快意自足的日子

直到一天

A Fallen Apple and Just a Folk Song

For my fellow student Ching-hang

1.
When an apple fell from its tree
Newton looked up and happened to see it
Seeing an apple fall from above, Newton thought,
I'm seeing an apple fall from above, what can I surmise?
I'm only seeing an apple fall from above
He was a little dispirited and hung his head
At that moment God happened to pass by
God passed by and saw the apple falling from the tree
God found that the manner of the apple falling was good and beautiful
As if for the first time he saw his own design
and creation
Moved beyond words, he decided to name his own mystery
and so, smiling, God stretched out his mischievous
adorable little(?) hand
to gently tap Newton's skull
and caught the apple that narrowly missed Newton's head
rolling it in front of Newton who began to understand
Everyone knows the story that came next
One Law after another was discovered
People lived happily and self-satisfied ever after

until one day

（二）
直到一天
有一詩人想
「如果落在牛頓腦袋的
不是蘋果」
噢
那會是甚麼

Just a little rain
falling all around . . .

一首民歌
合唱又獨唱

聽呀
Just a little rain
falling all around . . .
只是一些小雨
如果
落向牛頓腦袋的
不是蘋果

我們有理由相信
牛頓消失
和那些
燃燒着的
花草樹木
一樣

而幸好
上帝經過

2.
Until one day
there was a poet who thought,
If it wasn't an apple
that fell on Newton's head
Oh
what could it've been?

Just a little rain
falling all around . . .

A folk song
sung in unison or alone

Listen!
Just a little rain
falling all around . . .
Just some light rain
in case
what fell on Newton's head
wasn't an apple

We have reason to believe
Newton vanished
like those
incinerated
flowers
and trees

and fortunately
God passed by

幸好
我們的上帝
恰巧經過
上帝聽見
那歌聲
悲傷又哀傷
再一次
祂伸出
祂的手來

祂伸出
祂的手來
把雨點
接住
又——
把那些
雨點般
撞針
拔除

然後
一任
它們
輕柔地
灑落

灑落

在牛頓
並我們
此刻

Fortunately
our God
happened to pass by
and heard
the song
Sad and distressed
he stretched out
his hand
one more time

He stretched out
his hand
and caught
the raindrops
plucking
one by one
those
raindrop-like
firing pins

Then
he let
them
gently
scatter

scatter

on Newton
and on our
heads and our

喜極
而泣
的頭上
眼臉上

像音樂

像上帝的衪的嘆息的手指敲打的
你的　佢的

音樂

faces and eyes
weeping
ecstatically
in this moment

like music

like the lamenting tap of God's tap, tapping fingers
tapping your   tapping their

music

一首母親瑪利亞賴斯小姐之歌

給母親

賴斯小姐準備按掣的手重又放在琴鍵上
從加勒比海到黃海之濱
密西西比剛果河尼羅河
流淌着美妙的琴音
各地的人都用各各不同的聲音樂音jam進去
不同的節奏迴旋平行錯雜起伏流連
像眾手搓麵糰眾手整餅無酵或發酵
人們當然不知道賴斯小姐準備按掣的手
差一丁點兒碰觸那些大爆炸大裂變
上帝降臨對她這樣說
「之前我唔會同你講
之後都唔會
但當你按那掣之後
你唔好話上帝呀
我當時唔知道
縱使我現在證明
你確實唔知道」
這就是我們看見賴斯小姐
一路彈琴一路淚流滿面的原因
看到的人聽到的人感動不已因為
你知道嗎，朋友
母親瑪利亞這樣唱又這樣說
Let it be, let it be
每一個明日之後
總有一個明日之前
這彷彿是一個恩典
噢，這彷彿就是恩典

A Song from Mother Mary and Miss Condoleezza Rice

For my mother

Miss Rice's finger on the button is at the piano again
From the Caribbean to the shores of the Yellow Sea
to the Mississippi to the Congo to the Nile
the piano's lovely sounds surge forth
People all over the world *jam* in different voices and keys
Various rhythms spin, run in parallel, jumble, undulate and linger
like so many fingers kneading dough, so many fingers making leavened
    or unleavened bread
People don't know, of course, that Miss Rice's finger on the button
almost touched off those massive, explosive reactions
God had come down to say to her (in Cantonese),
I won't say a word to you
before or after
but when you press that button
don't say, 'O God,
I had no idea!'
even if I can prove now
that you really have no idea
This is why we catch sight of Miss Rice
playing the piano with her face covered in tears
and anyone who sees or hears her is moved because
you know, my friend,
Mother Mary sang and said,
Let it be, let it be
Every day after tomorrow
has a day before tomorrow—
if this isn't a kind of grace
Oh, if this isn't grace

偶成一二三

（一）
玉階生白露
for whom the bell tolls
我的心掛在樹上
（逗留在到來的離別之中）

你摘就是

（二）
菩提本無無
明鏡亦非非
本來無一一
何處惹哀哀

（三）
一個觀念暫作

有限被無限欣賞
無限被無限收藏

把你的名字寫在水上
日後好思量

Impromptu 123

1.
The jeweled steps are already quite white with dew
for whom the bell tolls
My heart hangs from a tree
(lingering in the arrival of a separation)

You have only to pick it

2.
The bodhi tree is not even nothing
The bright mirror is not never ever
From the beginning neither one nor another
Nowhere for sigh after sigh to gather

3.
A working concept:

The finite is infinitely admired
The infinite is infinitely archived

I write your name upon the water
to ponder in the future

伏匿匿躲貓貓練習曲 (1－6)

東平洲

（1）
地震來臨
我來跟你開玩笑
我未必跑得過地震
跑得過你
這就可以了

地震來臨
謝謝你來
跟我開玩笑

我不記得
有沒有
跟地震開玩笑
只記得
伏匿匿
躲貓貓
從1數到10

你在哪裏
你究竟在哪裏

千層岩
更樓石
海螺洞
難過水

Études No. 1–6 for Hide-and-Seek-Peekaboo

Tung Ping Chau Island

1.
An earthquake strikes
I come to joke around with you
I may not outrun the earthquake
but it's okay
as long as I can outrun you

An earthquake strikes
Thank you for coming
to joke around with me

I can't remember
if I joked around or not
with the earthquake
but I remember
hide-and-seek
peekaboo
counting from 1 to 10

Where are you
Where are you really

Thousand-Layer Cliff
Lookout Rock
Sea Conch Cave
Wave-Worn Pass

你在哪裏
你究竟在哪裏

（2）
你從平洲
搬到坪洲
就像地震

彷彿
就是地震

但謝謝你
無論我跑得多快
跑得多慢
以至跑不動了
你都回來
跟我開玩笑

天地空闊
沒有誰來
跟我開玩笑
除了你
從1數到10

（3）
地震來臨
地殼下陷

天地不仁
它跟自己

Where are you
Where are you really

2.
From Ping Chau Island
to Peng Chau Island
your move felt like an earthquake

as if
there had been an earthquake

But thank you
No matter how fast
or how slow I run
even if I'm not able to run anymore
you always come back
to joke around with me

In this expanse of heaven and earth
no one ever comes
to joke around with me
except for you
counting from 1 to 10

3.
An earthquake strikes
The earth's crust collapses

Heaven and earth are indifferent
They joke

開玩笑
這玩笑
就是地震
署大於地震

以至我們
跑得過地震
也跑不過這玩笑

從1數到10
乃有魚化石
乃有水成岩
乃有水成紋

（4）
地震來臨
或不來臨
你來就好
你來就是

有種喜悅
署大於珊瑚
漂木
珠蚌
海星星
千層石
豬籠草
摸盲雞
過家家
屋瓦上

with themselves
Their joke
is an earthquake
much larger than an earthquake

so that even though we
can outrun an earthquake
we can't outrun this joke

Counting from 1 to 10
and thus fish fossilize into stones
and thus water shapes sedimentary rock
and thus water shapes a thousand layers

4.
An earthquake strikes
or it doesn't strike
It's good if you come
Just come along

There's a kind of happiness
a little larger than coral
driftwood
pearls
starry starfish
thousand-layer rocks
pitcher plants
blind man's bluff
playing house
counting fireflies

螢火蟲
籐條下
受少少苦

從1數到10

有種喜悅
就像地震
署大於地震

（5）
謝謝你
從魚化石裏
走出來

從水成岩水成紋
你走出來

來被我看見
來被我逮住

我一生所繫
一生所等
惟
一
個
玩
笑
而
已

on a tiled roof
getting hit with a rattan switch
and suffering a little

Counting from 1 to 10

There's a happiness
like an earthquake
a little larger than an earthquake

5.
Thank you
Out of fossilized fish
you appeared

Out of sedimentary rock and thousands of layers
you appeared

to be seen by me
to be caught by me

All my life tied to
all my life waiting for
just
one
single
jo
ke
that's
all

誰的命運
躲避了誰的命運

又拍打了
誰的命運呢

（6）
伏匿匿躲貓貓

撿拾貝殼的手
撿取漂木的手
「要擁你入懷的手」

舉在虛空中的手

埋舟！

Whose fate
hid from someone else's fate

and tagged
the fate of another?

6.
Hide-and-seek-peekaboo

A hand picking up seashells
A hand collecting driftwood
A hand about to draw you close

A hand outstretched in the void

Olly olly oxen free!

灰欄記

布萊希特跨進欄內
決定誓不出來
我誓不出來
我誓不出來
當他念過了三遍
就一步跨出欄外
然後對自己
倒抽一口涼氣
幸甚幸甚
真是一額汗
欄內布萊希特
一頭霧水
欄都未劃完
灰都未刷
怎麼就
幸甚幸甚
走了出來呢
觀眾給弄糊塗了
才發覺自己原來
就是布萊希特
都爭湧闖進欄內
都爭湧走了出來
有時一頭霧水
有時一額汗
而通常的
那個圓
尚未刷灰

The Chalk Circle

Bertolt Brecht steps into a circle
and vows never to leave
I vow never to leave
I vow never to leave
He chants it three times
steps out of the circle
and with a chill down his spine
gasps at himself
I'm blest, I'm blest
That was a close shave!
The Bertolt Brecht in the circle
had his head in a fog
The circle is not yet sketched
The chalk mark is not yet drawn
So then why'd he say
I'm blest, I'm blest
and step out of the circle?
The audience is confused
only to realize that they themselves
are Bertolt Brecht
all rushing into the circle
all rushing out
sometimes with their heads in a fog
sometimes with a close shave
and that the usual
chalk circle
is not yet drawn

像是生母
更是養母
時而在圈內
時而在圈外
布萊希特
帶同觀眾
拉扯搬演
千禧年
大法官
那孩子
終將誕生
尚未誕生
捨不得誕生

They are like the birth mother
and the adoptive mother
at times in the circle
at times outside of the circle
Bertolt Brecht
leads the audience
in staging their pulling back and forth
as the chief judge
at the turn of the millennium
That child
who will be born
is not yet born
can't bear to be born

深河

全身而退的有福了
身體是他們的
那些未能全身而退

的人
的身體
都是他們的

深河之上
有沉默

深河之上
之下
有沉默

水藻
的嘆息

縈繞着的
水藻
的沉默

何必呢
它說

何必說呢
它說

Deep River

In the underworld, they gossip about the living
—Jaroslav Seifert

Blessed are those who escaped in one piece
as their bodies belong to themselves
The bodies of those who could not escape

in one piece
also belong
to those who did

Above the deep river
there's silence

Above the deep river
and under it
there's silence

The sigh
of algae

The lingering
silence
of algae

Why bother?
they say

Why bother to speak?
they say

又係嘭
佢話

又係嘭
佢話

有何必呢
的嘆息

有又係嘭
的沉默

六月將至
將息
的嘆息

年年五月
的沉默

生而為人
的沉默

我的燦爛

你的燦爛

佢的燦爛

歷史爭相押韻
This is just to say

說吧，沉默

Oh, right!
one says

Oh, right!
one says

There's the sigh
of *why bother*

There's the silence
of *oh, right!*

June approaches
The sighs
repose

May in silence
year after year

The silence
of being human

My splendor

Your splendor

Their splendor

Histories compete to rhyme
This is just to say

speak up, silence!

湊湊靜默之修行

「不要總體化、不要簡單化、不要阻擋他的步伐、不要使軌跡凝固不變、不要追求某種優勢、不要抹殺事物也不要抹平，尤其不要做自私的打算，不要據為己有或重新據為己有（即使是通過那種名為拒絕而實為打算借此達到重新據為己有之目的的悖論形式），不要佔用過去和現在從來都不可能據為己有的東西。」

——雅克・德里達，於路易・阿圖塞喪禮上的發言。（轉摘自鄧小樺Ticklish網誌）

因真理
得自由
以服務
你撐起一把傘
我就盡想着這些了
有人叫耶穌做和尚
洋和尚洋和尚
叫他做和尚洋和尚
有甚麼關係呢
眾所周知
又眾所不知
他說
革命
就是修行
認識了別人的好
照見自己的良善
帶髮
不帶髮
有甚麼關係呢

Tagging along with the Ascetic Practice of Silence

*"... not to totalize or simplify, not to immobilize him or fix a
trajectory, not to seek some advantage, not to cancel things out or try
to get even, and especially not to calculate, not to appropriate or
reappropriate (even if it be through that paradoxical form of
manipulating or calculating reappropriation called rejection), not to
take hold of what was inappropriable and must remain so."*

—Jacques Derrida, statement read at Louis Althusser's
funeral (quoted from Tang Siu-wa's blog *Ticklish*)

The truth
will set you free
To serve
you hold up an umbrella
This is what I've been thinking
Some call Jesus a lama
a western lama a western lama
Calling him a lama or a western lama
what's the difference?
As everyone knows
and no one knows
he said
revolution
is an ascetic practice
Understanding other people's goodness
reflects your own kindness
A shaved head
or an unshaved head—
what's the difference?

五餅二魚
又五餅二魚
五餅二魚
撐一把傘
然後又一把傘
又一把傘
像一個走在人群中孤獨的和尚
他說
仇與友
愛者與不愛者
革命
是修行
一步
一腳印

黃金
黃金

依家冇
將來都冇

革命
是一種
修行

認識到
自己
的好
照見
別人
的良善

Five loaves and two fish
and five loaves and two fish
five loaves and two fish
Holding up an umbrella
then another umbrella
and another umbrella
Like a solitary lama walking in a crowd
he said
enemies and friends,
the loved and the unloved,
revolution
is an ascetic practice
One footprint
for every step

Gold
Gold

None now
nor in the future

Revolution
is a kind
of ascetic practice

The understanding
that your own
goodness
reflects
other people's
kindness

並種種
救贖
的可能

像走在人群中
孤獨的和尚
他說

他對他
自己說

革命
是永恆慘烈的一種
不斷放棄權力的鬥爭

and every
possibility
of redemption

Like a solitary lama
walking in a crowd
he said

He said
to himself

Revolution
is a kind of eternally devastating struggle
of forever renouncing power

Notes

We use the Hanyu Pinyin system without diacritical marks to render most Chinese words; however, when an expression is in Cantonese, we follow the Yale romanization system with diacritical marks. Translations are ours unless otherwise indicated.

Daily Life

Both of Yam Gong's poetry collections (1997; 2010) begin with this poem. The line "wailed for my soul's return" is based on the Cantonese term *haam gēng* (喊驚), which means "wailing for the frightened," and refers to a traditional religious ritual performed in China that entails wailing in order to call back the frightened soul of an ill child believed to be taken by an evil spirit.

Reclamation

The reclaimed land refers to an area in Hong Kong where Shun Tak Center and the Hong Kong–Macau Ferry Terminal are now located. The reclamation began in 1958, and the area was widely known as a "night club for common people." The "club" eventually moved westward after the Shun Tak Center and Hong Kong–Macau Ferry Terminal were built, and by the 1990s, it had disappeared.

According to Yam Gong, the Flute King and Mr. Lively Ghost No.7 were real street musicians he encountered during his youth.

Zhou Xuan (ca. 1920–57), nicknamed "Golden Voice," was an iconic, short-lived Chinese singer and film actress who became famous in the 1930s.

The phrase *"a dozen pains"* is based on a term from traditional Chinese medicine that means, literally, "five strains and seven impairments:" *wu lao qi shang* (五勞七傷).

"Down-and-out scholars" refers to a stock character in classical Chinese romances and operas. Before passing the imperial exam to attain a position in the bureaucracy, he was not "qualified" to marry his beloved.

The image of *"dried husks / sinking and large stones bobbing"* is taken from a Chinese prediction said to have been written by the military strategist Liu Bowen (1311–75). In Chinese, the word for "husk" matches the sound of the first character in the name of the Chinese political reformer Kang Youwei (1858–1927), and the word for "stone" matches the sound of the last character of the military leader and statesman Chiang Kai-shek (1887–1975). The prediction is considered to be accurate because Kang Youwei's fate eventually sank, whereas Chiang Kai-shek rose to great heights. This story was commonly known when Yam Gong was growing up.

The poem alludes to a folk legend about two famous military advisers in Chinese history, Zhuge Liang (181–234) and Liu Bowen (1311–75). According to the legend as recounted by Yam Gong, in order to challenge the long-dead Zhuge Liang, considered the smartest person in Chinese history, Liu Bowen went to dismantle Zhuge Liang's ancestral hall. Upon tearing down a wooden plaque, he saw that it was inscribed with Zhuge Liang's words: "Five hundred years ago, I knew about you / Who in the future do you know today?"

"The endless waves never washed away . . ." is a reversal of the poetic image of waves washing away the memories of ancient heroes in the Song dynasty poem "Cherishing the Past at Red Cliff" (赤壁懷古) by Su Shi (1037–1101): "The great river departs eastward: / Its waves have washed away, / Dashing men of a thousand ages." Michael A. Fuller, *An Introduction to Chinese Poetry From the Canon of Poetry to the Lyrics of the Song Dynasty* (Cambridge, MA: Harvard University Press, 2017), 397.

Shek Tong Tsui was a red light district in Hong Kong that flourished from the early 1900s until 1935, when brothels were prohibited in Hong Kong. "Tiny Su" is a rendering of the name "Su Xiaoxiao" ("Little Su"), a legendary Chinese courtesan frequently depicted in stories and poems.

The phrase "Ah, this life" evokes the ending of the poem "Life" (生涯) by the mainland Chinese poet Xin Di (1912–2004).

On the Margins
The line "often cutting past me" attempts to capture the Chinese idiom *pitou pi nao* (劈頭劈腦), which means "right on the head," often with a violent connotation.

Literally, the characters mean "chopping a head, chopping a brain."

"A wet black bough" is from Ezra Pound's poem "In a Station of the Metro." In the closing lines of the Chinese poem, instead of the proper measure word *ye* (頁, "sheet") for a poster, Yam Gong uses a character with the same sound, but which means "leaf."

The Salted Fish Shop (A Sonnet)
"So handsome" (*rouzhibinbin*, 肉質彬彬) is a play on a Chinese phrase, *wenzhibinbin* (文質彬彬), that describes someone who is gentle and refined, combining the characters *wen* (文, "outward grace") with *zhi* (質, "inner worth") in a "harmonious balance" (*binbin*, 彬彬). Yam Gong changes the first character, *wen* ("outward grace"), to *rou* (肉, "meat"), so his new phrase implies the pleasing texture of fish.

And So You Look at Festival Lights along the Street
The epigraph is from the opening lines of Du Fu's poem "To Wei Ba in Retirement" (贈衛八處士), in which the speaker sees an old friend after more than twenty years and meets his children. The first three lines are adapted from Stephen Owen's translation of the poem, "Presented to the Recluse Wei," *The Poetry of Du Fu*, vol.1 (Boston: De Gruyter, 2016), 73, and the phrase "Scorpius and Orion" is adopted from Steve Bradbury's translation, "To Wei Ba in Retirement," in *Beacons* 10 (2008): 37. The fourth line is Yam Gong's invention.

The Subway
In January 1984, roughly 200 members of the Mass Transit Railway (MTR) Operating Department Staff Union, made up largely of train drivers, went on strike to demand recognition of their union and procedures for negotiating work policies. Members from six other unions in Hong Kong, including the Wharf Workers Union, joined in support. The three-day strike was resolved when the MTR Corporation agreed to the union's demands. In April of the same year, drivers went on strike again with less success: fourteen workers, including the union's chairman, were dismissed by the MTR Corporation.

The Sinful Swan

Published in 1982, this poem cites specific places and events in Hong Kong. For instance, the poem mentions an argument about a skybridge related to the Mandarin Oriental Hotel. The "wooden tea house" refers to the Luk Yu Tea House. The second stanza references the Yau Ma Tei "boat people," who were fighting their relocation on land by the colonial government during the late 1970s.

"You got it wrong" is based on the Cantonese phrase *gáau cho* (搞錯), meaning to make a mistake or to mix up, and can imply frustration.

Back Pain

The line "seven times seven equals forty-nine days of the dead" refers to "doing the sevenths" (做七), a Chinese funeral ritual stemming from Buddhism and Taoism.

Quiet Night Thoughts

The title and the final lines allude to the famous poem "Quiet Night Thoughts" (靜夜思) by Li Bai (701–62): "Bright moonlight shining before my bed / I thought it was frost on the ground / Raising my head, I gaze at the bright moon / lowering my head, I think of home" (床前明月光 / 疑是地上霜 / 舉頭望明月 / 低頭思故鄉). Our version is adapted from Charles Egan's translation in *How to Read Chinese Poetry: A Guided Anthology*, ed. Zong-Qi Cai (New York: Columbia University Press, 2008), 210.

The lines "I'm like the boy who made a secret hole in his wall to get more light, / peeping beyond the starry sky" invokes an idiom that means "boring a hole in the wall to steal more light" (鑿壁偷光) based on the Chinese story of a boy named Kuang Heng. By boring a hole in his wall to "steal" light from his neighbor, he could study more at night.

Airplane olives (飛機欖) were a street snack (pickled olives) thrown up to people on their balconies or through their windows. They were popular in Hong Kong between the 1950s and 1970s, when apartment buildings were comparatively low.

A "funeral horn," also known as a "suona horn," is a double-reed wind instrument.

"Leading mourners processing on and on" is an adaptation of the first line ("On and on, always on and on") of an anonymous Han dynasty poem, "Life-Parting," trans. Arthur Waley, in *Classical Chinese Literature: An Anthology of Translations, Volume 1: From Antiquity to the Tang Dynasty*, eds. John Minford and Joseph S.M. Lau (New York: Columbia University Press and The Chinese University Press of Hong Kong, 2000), 392.

The subsequent line "Chance encounters between those who've never met—" adapts language from "Ballad of the Pipa Lute" (琵琶行), by the Tang dynasty poet Bai Juyi (772–846): "Both of us hapless outcasts at the farther end of the sky; meeting like this, why must we be old friends to understand one another?" (同是天涯淪落人 / 相逢何必曾相識). "Song of the Lute," trans. Burton Watson, in *Classical Chinese Literature: An Anthology of Translations, Volume 1: From Antiquity to the Tang Dynasty*, eds. John Minford and Joseph S. M. Lau (New York: Columbia University Press and The Chinese University of Hong Kong, 2000), 893.

Yam Gong alludes to a Chinese fairytale called "The Rats Marrying Off Their Daughter" (*Laoshu Jia Nu*, 老鼠嫁女). Although the story has many versions, it is generally about a mother and father rat who try to marry off their young daughter, and in their misguided ambition to match her with someone powerful, finally settle on a cat, who eats his bride on their wedding day.

The "figurine man" refers to hawkers on the street who made intricate figures out of glutinous rice.

An Occasion
This poem evokes a famous Zen (*Chan*) story about enlightenment: "The Chan master Qingyuan Weixin of Jizhou ascended the high seat and said: 'Thirty years ago, before this old monk had begun to practice *chan*, I saw mountains as mountains and rivers as rivers. Then later on I came face to face with a teacher and made some headway, and I saw that mountains are not mountains and rivers are not rivers. But now, having reached a place of rest, I once again see that mountains are just mountains and rivers are just rivers. To all of you I ask, as for these three ways of understanding, are they the same or are they different? Should there be a monastic or layperson among you who can find a way out of this, I will acknowledge your having come face to face with this old monk.'" Translation by Robert H. Sharf, "Chan Cases," in *What Can't Be Said: Paradox and*

Contradiction in East Asian Thought, eds. Yasuo Deguchi, Jay L. Garfield, Robert H. Sharf, and Graham Priest (New York: Oxford University Press, 2021), 80.

A Butterfly Flaps Its Wings
The epigraph for this poem was invented by Yam Gong. The poem appears to allude to General Hua of the Tang dynasty featured in the 1932 short story collection *The General's Head* (將軍底頭) by the Shanghai writer Shi Zhecun (1905–2003). In the story, the general is decapitated on the battlefield, but he doesn't realize his head is gone until he hears his love interest teasing him, and then he collapses immediately.

According to the *Classics of Mountains and Seas*, Xingtian (刑天) is the demigod of Chinese mythology who was decapitated by a rival god, but who continued to fight as a headless body. His nipples became his eyes and his navel turned into his mouth.

Yu Lai-zhen (1923–2004) was a famous Hong Kong actress. In the 1957 film *The Headless Empress Bears a Son* (無頭東宮生太子), she portrayed an empress who gave birth to a son just before she was beheaded and, as a ghost, still cared for him.

The Chinese idiom *guomu bu wang* (過目不忘) means "to have a photographic memory," but Yam Gong changes the third character of the expression to reverse its meaning, which we render as "Uncommitted / to memory."

The Auntie Who Offered Water (A Story from My Mother)
The poem mentions several times the influential modern Chinese writer Lu Xun (1881–1936). The epigraph, for instance, adapts language from Lu Xun's essay "What Is Required to Be a Father Today" (我們現在怎麼做父親), which is included in his collection *Grave* (墳).

Yam Gong twists a Chinese idiom referring to the image of bringing the Buddha to the West (*song fu song dao xi*, 送佛送到西), which implies the idea of not stopping halfway in a good deed.

"Kuaiji" is an old name for the region now known as Zhejiang province.

The phrase "Dear onlookers" is based on the Chinese term *kanguan* (看官), an expression used by street storytellers to address their audiences.

Regarding the last line, Yam Gong includes an endnote in his 2010 book: "The 'XX' brand name is still undecided—sincerely asking for advertisements."

Collected Poems from the King of Laziness (4 Selections)
The phrase "King of Laziness" refers to *sèh wòhng* (蛇王), literally, "snake king," Cantonese slang for being lazy, or taking a break at work without permission. *Sèh* or "snake" (蛇) has a similar sound as a Cantonese word (*se*, 卸) meaning "to slack off."

Startling Hair
This poem shares the same title of the titular poem in a book by the Hong Kong poet Wong Leung-wo (1963–).

Exercises in Fireworks (20)
The stanza about thorn birds reminded us of an old Chinese story about an unhappy king who lost his kingdom, became a cuckoo bird, and sang for so long that he bled from his mouth. The blood turned into azaleas. However, Yam Gong confirmed that the stanza is inspired by the 1983 television drama *The Thorn Birds*.

The phrase "blood-sweating horse from heaven" references the now-extinct Ferghana horse from Central Asia.

"Spraying water in new-year celebration" refers to Songkran, a water festival celebrated at the New Year in southeast Asian countries, especially Thailand.

In Chinese folklore, the gods punished Wu Gang by making him endlessly cut down a self-healing osmanthus tree on the moon. There are different accounts of the reason for Wu Gang's punishment.

According to the Chinese legend, Chang'e stole an elixir from her husband that made her immortal. She escaped the earth and became an exiled goddess of the moon.

I Have Cheeks
Yam Gong's footnote from his 2010 collection: "When my daughter was young, I coaxed her to kiss her father. No kissing!, she said. Come kiss dad. No kissing!, she said. No one's kissing Dad, so Dad has to kiss himself—he has to smooch

himself, I said. This is my mouth, this is my face. I spun my head and mouth around, trying to chase and kiss my spinning face. The faster my head spun, the more my daughter laughed. She laughed and laughed, and my head spun and spun, and I ended up with this sad poem."

Blind Drifting

The Chinese term *mangliu* (盲流, literally, "blind drifting") is a shortened form of *mangmu liudong* (盲目流動), a pejorative term that refers to undocumented migrants from the countryside in mainland China who move to the cities for new opportunities. We use the phrase "blind drifting" to broaden the meaning of the term in concert with Yam Gong's poem.

"Ornamentations and talismanic scripts," or *fulu* (符籙), are incantations and symbols that may be written or painted on a charm or an amulet by Daoist practitioners.

"Drifting toward a death foretold" alludes to the novella *Chronicle of a Death Foretold* by Gabriel García Márquez (1927–2014).

Méditation

"Ah Yu" is Agrado, a transgender sex worker in Pedro Almodóvar's film *All About My Mother* (1999). Yam Gong has noted that the epigraph is adapted from the caption of a photo of the Italian porn star-turned-politician Ilona Staller, "Cicciolina," in an issue of *Penthouse* magazine.

The title refers to an intermezzo from the 1894 French opera *Thaïs* by composer Jules Massenet (1842–1912). The opera is based on Anatole France's 1890 novel by the same name, itself a retelling of the story of St. Thaïs (ca. 4th century). The story follows a monk who tries to save the soul of Thaïs, a beautiful courtesan in fourth-century Alexandria, but in the process of converting her to Christianity, he falls passionately in love with her. Renouncing his beliefs, the monk rushes back to the convent where he had taken her for penance, but he arrives too late: Thaïs has been declared a saint by the nuns, and now she is dying. Although he confesses his love for her on her deathbed—"nothing is true but life and the love of human beings"—she cannot see him, for she is dying with a vision of angels welcoming her.

The line "and when you learned about the Way in the morning" is based on a line from Confucius about enlightenment: "Once you learn of the Dao in the morning, you can die in the evening without regrets."

The repetition of "nameless river" in the final lines is a rendering of *māt séui* (乜水, literally, "what water?"), which is impolite Cantonese slang for "who are you?," possibly because the Cantonese pronunciation of "water" resembles the word "who" (*sèuih,* 誰). Yam Gong makes poetic use of this Cantonese phrase by contextualizing *māt séui* to resemble the way of naming a river in classical Chinese.

Moving a Stone
The last stanza combines language from 1 Corinthians 13:4 ("Love is patient, love is kind . . .") and 1 Corinthians 13:13 ("So faith, hope, love remain, these three; but the greatest of these is love.")

Performance Art
The "decapitation" of Edvard Eriksen's bronze statue *The Little Mermaid* in Copenhagen took place on January 6, 1998. It had been decapitated before, on April 24, 1942; its right arm was sawn off on July 22, 1984.

The fourth stanza ("like the Sirens / in a time of silence / with those seven kinds / of singing") evokes the 1997 short story collection *Seven Kinds of Silence* (七種靜默), by the Hong Kong writer Wong Bik-wan (1961–). In the title story of her book, Wong writes, "The sin of God is silence. If there are seven types of sin, God has seven types of silence" (上帝之罪，在沉默無言。如果有七宗罪，上帝就有七種靜默). Wong Bik-wan, *Seven Kinds of Silence* (Hong Kong: Cosmos, 1997), 337.

An Entryway / A Resting Place
This poem alludes to the same Zen story of enlightenment found in "An Occasion."

The narrator is recalling his mother's bedtime story about a man telling a story on a boat. Hence, the line of dialogue, *"Deep in the mountains, there was an old sparrow—,"* is spoken by the man, as recounted by the mother.

"With not a single pube" refers to vulgar Cantonese slang (*mòuh dōu móuh tiuh*, 毛都冇條) that means "there's nothing there," or, literally, "not a single piece of hair," where hair has an obscene connotation.

"Dense willows and bright flowers" (*liu'anhuaming*, 柳暗花明) is our rendering of a Chinese idiom with the hopeful sense that after walking for a long time one will eventually come upon a village emerging through the willow trees and flowers. It appears in the poem "A Trip to West Mountain Village" (遊山西村) by the Southern Song dynasty poet Lu You (1125–1209). See Burton Watson's translation in *The Columbia Book of Chinese Poetry: From Early Times to the Thirteenth Century* (New York: Columbia University Press, 1984), 315.

The Third Bank
The title evokes João Guimarães Rosa's short story "The Third Bank of the River," published in *Primeiras Estorias (First Stories)* in 1962. The story describes a father who, without explanation, decides to live alone on a boat in the middle of a river.

According to Yam Gong's footnote on the poem when it was first published in the 2002 issue of *Poetry Network* (詩網絡), the lines "As a result . . . // Because . . . // Although . . . // Despite . . ." (多虧…… // 因為…… // 然而……// 儘管……) are from Chen Li's (1954–) Chinese translation of "Could Have" by Wislawa Szymborska (1923–2012). Our English version is borrowed from Stanislaw Baranczak and Clare Cavanagh's translation in *View With a Grain of Sand: Selected Poems* (New York: Harcourt, 1995), 65. Yam Gong also noted that the line "clinking   and clanking" is borrowed from a poem called "The Streets of Hung Hom: Staircases and Poems" (紅磡的街道：樓梯與詩歌) by the Hong Kong poet Leung Chi-wah (1966–).

A Fox's Tale in Seven Parts
In Chinese mythology, "fox spirits" (*hulijing*, 狐狸精) could transform into human forms, often as a beautiful woman who enchants a man.

According to Yam Gong, this poem was inspired by the 1986 French film *37° 2 le matin* (*Betty Blue* in English).

The first line of the epigraph ("Touched by your glance back") is similar to a line from the poem "Song of a Girl in an Upper Storey" (樓上女兒曲) by the Tang dynasty poet Lu Tong (790–835): "because I'm touched by your affectionate glance back" (直緣感君恩愛一回顧). The second line ("returning home in evening snow") is taken from the last line of a classical Chinese quatrain called "Lodging with the Recluse of Hibiscus Mountain on a Snowy Evening" (逢雪宿芙蓉山主人) by the Tang dynasty poet Liu Changqing (ca. 710–ca. 789).

Somewhere . . .

Yam Gong informed us that the rock imagery is derived from Palestinians fighting Israelis with slingshots.

The Chinese poem borrows two lines from Jacques Prévert's poem "Barbara:" *Toi que je ne connaissais pas / Toi qui ne me connaissais pas.* We adopt Lawrence Ferlinghetti's translation: "You whom I didn't know / You who didn't know me." Jacques Prévert, *Paroles: Selected Poems*, trans. Lawrence Ferlinghetti (San Francisco: City Lights Books, 2001), 113.

Found Object (Urinal)

"Ah Shek" refers to Yam Gong's son.

The phrases *niao niao* (尿尿, pee-pee) and *niao niao* (鳥鳥, wee-wee) rhyme in Chinese and resemble baby talk.

The Chinese word for "bird" is slang for "penis."

Plugging Your Ears to Steal a Bell

The Chinese title is an idiom meaning "to deceive oneself," i.e., covering your ears while you steal a bell, as if no one will hear you.

Rubbing Black Bean Sauce on a Pomfret

The third stanza alludes to a couplet written in Chinese at the door of St. Michael's Catholic Cemetery in Hong Kong.

Menghanyao (蒙汗藥), rendered here as "love potion," is believed to be a concoction of jimson weed used to sedate someone, often for sexual purposes. It appears frequently in classical Chinese fiction and martial arts (*wuxia*) stories. An endnote in Yam Gong's 2010 collection explains that when a friend steamed a fresh, delicious fish, Yam Gong's poet friends pointed at the fish, as if they regretted not having a chance to use their own hands to rub black bean sauce on it. He added, "Amid being tipsy, a poem emerged, and amid this poem, a fish emerged." Fish in Chinese have a sexual connotation, such as the idiom *yushui zhi huan* (魚水之歡, literally, "the joy of fish in water").

A Fallen Apple and Just a Folk Song
Dedicated to Hong Kong poet Matthew Cheng Ching-hang (1981–).

According to an endnote in Yam Gong's 2010 collection, the lines *"If it wasn't an apple / that fell on Newton's head"* is from the book *If It Wasn't an Apple that Fell on Newton's Head* (如果落向牛頓腦袋的不是蘋果) by the Hong Kong poet Ho Fuk-yan (ca. 1950–).

In modern written Chinese, *ta* (祂) is the genderless, personal pronoun for God. We resort to the male pronoun "he" to clarify who's speaking.

In Cantonese, *kéuih* (佢) is the third person singular pronoun for both genders. We use a plural pronoun ("their") to avoid distinguishing a gender.

The poem quotes lines in English from "What Have They Done to the Rain" (1962), a protest song against nuclear testing made famous by Joan Baez (1941–): "Just a little rain falling all around, / The grass lifts its head to the heavenly sound, / Just a little rain, just a little rain, / What have they done to the rain?" The lyrics were written by Malvina Reynolds (1900–78).

Impromptu 123
Yam Gong's 2010 book has an endnote for this poem: "'Impromptu 1' is a *jiju* [a poem made of lines by others]: Li Bai, John Donne, and Paul Éluard, respectively. The phrase in parenthesis in the fourth line is from Heidegger. 'I write your name upon the water' is from John Keats." Our translation borrows Ezra Pound's version of the first line of "The Jewel Stairs' Grievance" by Li Bai. The matching line from Paul Éluard's "Poèmes" (*Le cœur sur l'arbre vous n'aviez qu'à le cueillir*) is adapted from a translation by Renée Riese Hubert: "That heart on the tree, you had only to gather it." Renée Riese Hubert, *Surrealism and the Book* (Berkeley: University of California Press, 1988), 58.

Section two is a rewriting of a famous Buddhist verse by the Zen monk Huineng (638–713):

> The bodhi is in fact not a tree
> The bright mirror has no stand
> Everything is nothing
> What's left to gather dust?

Yam Gong's version cut the last character in the first three lines of the original poem and doubled the penultimate character, so that each line ends in an abstraction. In the final line, he replaced the last two characters by matching the sound of the last character with a new character that he doubled, changing the last word of the poem from "dust" to "sorrow."

Huineng's poem was in response to a verse by Shen Xiu (ca. 606–705):

> The body is the bodhi tree
> The mind is like a bright mirror's stand
> At each moment make sure it's clean
> And don't let it gather dust

The translations are from Lucas Klein's *The Organization of Distance: Poetry, Translation, Chineseness* (Leiden: Brill Press, 2018), 148–49.

Études No. 1–6 for Hide-and-Seek-Peekaboo
The Chinese title contains both the Cantonese word *buhk nēi nēi* (伏匿匿) and the Mandarin word *duo mao mao* (躲貓貓) for "hide-and-seek." We use "Hide-and-Seek-Peekaboo" to capture the unusual doubling in the title.

Tung Ping Chau is an uninhabited island in Hong Kong known for its geological formations.

The Chalk Circle
The Caucasian Chalk Circle by Bertolt Brecht (1898–1956) was inspired by *The Chalk Circle* (灰闌記) by Li Qianfu, a Yuan dynasty playwright. Early in Brecht's play, the "Singer" character says of the play-within-a play, "It's called 'The Chalk Circle' and comes from the Chinese. But we'll do it, of course, in a changed version."

Bertolt Brecht, *The Caucasian Chalk Circle*, trans. Eric Bentley (New York: Grove Press, 1966), 25.

Deep River
The epigraph is attributed to the Czech poet Josef Hora (1892–1945) by Jaroslav Seifert (1901–86) in his memoir *All the Beauties of the World*.

Tagging along with the Ascetic Practice of Silence
"Tagging along" refers to the Chinese term *courenao* (湊熱鬧), which means, roughly, "to join a bustling crowd." Yam Gong replaced the word for "bustling crowd" with a phrase meaning "the ascetic practice of silence."

The English translation of the epigraph is from Pascale-Anne Brault and Michael Naas, *The Work of Mourning* (Chicago: University of Chicago Press, 2003), 116.

Acknowledgments

We approach translation as an iterative, collaborative effort, and we are deeply grateful to the many people who have assisted us along the way, including Carrie Olivia Adams, Steve Bradbury, Natascha Bruce, Mignon Chiu Wai-yee, Mimi Chun, Jeffery Clapp, Michael Earl Craig, Jennifer Feeley, Eleanor Goodman, Nathan Hoks, Daniel Howe, Lucas Klein, Jennifer Kronovet, Suzanne Lai Tsui-yan, Stuart Lau, Louise Law, Jacqueline Leung, Sandra Lim, Andrea Lingenfelter, Trey Moody, Marco Ng Chun-yin, Collier Nogues, Caryl Pagel, Zeb Raft, Kaitlin Reese, Katy Scrogin, Parker Smathers, So Wai-nam, Chris Song, Tang Siu-wa, Jeremy Tiang, Madeleine Thien, Diane To, Christophe Tong, John Wakefield, Grace Wong, Nicholas Wong, Yeung Tong-lung, Kyoko Yoshida, and Zhang Hongsheng. We are especially grateful to Yvonne Yevan Yu, who served as an "essential worker" on this project with her deliberate readings and insightful suggestions. We also wish to thank the Hong Kong Arts Development Council, National Endowment for the Arts, and the Tomaž Šalamun Poetry Centre (Ljubljana) for their timely support, as well as the Faculty of Arts at Hong Kong Baptist University. We remain profoundly thankful to Christopher Mattison and the team at Zephyr Press, and, of course, to Yam Gong himself, as he patiently entertained our questions on Peng Chau Island.

Grateful acknowledgment is made to the following publications in which some of our translations first appeared, often in earlier versions:

Brick (Summer 2020): "I Have Cheeks," "Found Object (Urinal)"
jubilat (Spring 2021): "Daily Life," "Back Pain"
Asymptote's Translation Tuesday (Summer 2021): "The Salted Fish Shop (A Sonnet)"
Kenyon Review (Summer 2021): "Exercises in Fireworks (20)," "*Collected Poems from the King of Laziness* (4 Selections)"
Past the Horizon, Hong Kong International Photo Festival (Summer 2021): "The Third Bank," "Performance Art," "Impromptu 123," "A Song from Mother Mary and Miss Condoleezza Rice"

Paperbag (Summer 2021): "Standing an Egg on a Stone Table, "A Fox's Tale in Seven Parts," "Deep River"

The Margins/Transpacific Literary Project, Asian American Writers' Workshop (Summer 2021): "An Occasion"

Chinese Literature Today (Fall 2021): "Just Come Along," "Mute Wish," "Méditation," "Rubbing Black Bean Sauce on a Pomfret," "The Braking Bus"

The Canary (Fall 2021): "And So You Look at Festival Lights along the Street," "Blind Drifting"

Two Lines (Fall 2021): "Waiting for '97 and Godot," "Flying Ants Approaching Water"

Sand (Fall 2021): "The Subway"

Fonograph Editions (Spring 2022): "Reclamation"

Contributor Bios

Born in 1949, **Yam Gong**, the pen name of Lau Yee-ching, is a celebrated Hong Kong poet whose honors include the Hong Kong Youth Literature Award, the Workers' Literature Award, and the Hong Kong Biennial Award for Chinese Literature for his first book *And So You Look at Festival Lights along the Street* (1997). He later published an extended edition of this collection, titled *And So Moving a Stone You Look at Festival Lights along the Street* (2010). Appointed to the juries of several awards in Hong Kong, including the Qui Ying Poetry Award and the Lee Sing-wah Modern Poetry Award, he has been invited to the International Poetry Nights in Hong Kong, the Macau Literary Festival, and the Taipei Poetry Festival, among others.

James Shea is the author of two poetry collections, *The Lost Novel* and *Star in the Eye*, both from Fence Books. Recipient of grants from the Fulbright U.S. Scholar Program, Hong Kong Arts Development Council, and National Endowment for the Arts, he is the director of the Creative and Professional Writing Program at Hong Kong Baptist University.

Dorothy Tse is a Hong Kong fiction writer whose books include *Owlish* and *So Black*. Tse has received the Hong Kong Book Prize, Unitas New Fiction Writers' Award (Taiwan), and the Hong Kong Award for Creative Writing in Chinese. She has been a resident at Art Omi, the University of Iowa's International Writing Program, and the Vermont Studio Center.